Barbie® DOLL
AROUND THE WORLD

IDENTIFICATION
&
VALUES
1964 – 2007

J. Michael Augustyniak

COLLECTOR BOOKS
A Division of Schroeder Publishing Co., Inc.

On the cover Info — clockwise: 1991 Dream Bride Barbie from Europe, 1998 Flores De Mayo Reyna Elena Barbie from the Philipines, 1997 Sohni Punjab Di Barbie from India, 1984 Kimomo Barbie from Japan, 1999 Kebaya Barbie from Malaysia, 1984 A Boneca Que E Uma Estrela Barbie from Brazil, 2006 French Maid Barbie from Canada.

Cover design by Beth Summers
Book design by Christen Byrd
Cover photography by Charles R. Lynch

COLLECTOR BOOKS
P.O. Box 3009
Paducah, Kentucky 42002-3009

www.collectorbooks.com

Copyright © 2008 J. Michael Augustyniak

The current values in this book should be used only as a guide. They are not intended to set prices, which vary from one section of the country to another. Auction prices as well as dealer prices vary greatly and are affected by condition as well as demand. Neither the author nor the publisher assumes responsibility for any losses that might be incurred as a result of consulting this guide.

Searching for a Publisher?
We are always looking for people knowledgeable within their fields. If you feel that there is a real need for a book on your collectible subject and have a large comprehensive collection, contact Collector Books.

Proudly printed and bound in the
United States of America

Contents

Preface

Barbie doll is currently sold in over 140 countries around the world. With nearly 1.7 billion children under the age of 14 in the world, the United States is home to only 3.4 percent of the world's children. Mattel has even changed her face to appeal to the buyers in foreign lands, so Barbie doll in 2007 is as diverse as the peoples of the earth. This book is dedicated to the foreign children of the world who will become tomorrow's Barbie doll collectors.

Introduction

Mattel U.S. has teased American collectors for years by gifting conventioneers with foreign-market Barbie dolls not sold in the U.S. At the 1985 national Barbie convention in Michigan, Mattel's gift doll to conventioneers was the Takara Japanese Traditional Style Barbie wearing a kimono. In 1989 Mattel U.S. gifted conventioneers in California with Passeio Viky dolls imported from Brazil, and in 1990 conventioneers attending the national convention in Texas received the Friendship Barbie doll, commemorating the reunification of Germany. If American collectors were not already intrigued with foreign-market Barbie dolls, they were now.

Australia

The land down under has seen some unique and valuable Barbie dolls. While Australia and Europe have typically shared the same dolls since Australia is a former colony of England, some notable exceptions include vintage early 1970s "dressed box" dolls featuring inexpensive Barbie dolls wearing fashions that were previously available separately as boxed or carded fashions. Barbie doll even wore an Australian Olympic swimsuit for the 1976 Olympic games, and her gold medal appropriately featured a kangaroo! More recently, Australia has garnered attention for its shared exclusive with Europe, the Silkstone Nurse Barbie.

Canada

Our neighbor to the north has long been the source of Barbie dolls not available in the U.S. Many of the wonderful European-market Barbie dolls since the mid-1970s have also been available in Canada; to avoid duplication and for ease in arranging series, the dolls shared by Canada and Europe are found in the chapter on Europe, and only those dolls available solely in Canada are shown in the chapter on Canada. Canadian exclusives include numerous "dressed box" Barbie dolls wearing discontinued fashions or fashions previously worn by earlier dolls, dolls participating in the 1976 and 1988 Olympic games, and Canada's most famous celebrity among Barbie doll collectors, hockey great Wayne Gretzky. More recently, Inuit Legend Barbie has showcased Canada's rich heritage, and the Silkstone French Maid Barbie has given American collectors the most celebrated Canadian exclusive to date. Mattel Canada has further encouraged Canadian Barbie doll collecting by sponsoring the first Canadian national Barbie doll convention, held in Alberta in September 2006.

Europe

Europe has been a treasure trove of unique foreign Barbie dolls since the mid-1960s. From unique versions of the American Girl Barbie with bendable legs to the legendary German Francie, Europe has produced the most desirable foreign-market Barbie family dolls for over four decades. Barbie doll's tiny twin siblings Tutti and Todd were revived in the early 1970s in Europe, and their world expanded greatly until 1980. While Malibu Barbie boasted a dark brown suntan in the U.S. in the 1970s, her swimsuit-wearing contemporary Funtime Barbie had pale white skin in Europe, perhaps due to the rainy climate! Europeans loved the glamour and glitz of SuperStar Barbie, so many dressed box versions of the doll were sold there in the late 1970s and early 1980s. Europe has also been the source of name idiosyncrasies; when the American Black Barbie sold in 1980 made history as the first African-American Barbie, the identical doll sold in Europe was called Ebony Christie! Even Barbie doll's tiny sister Kelly is known by another name in Europe — she is called Shelly there.

An active adult Barbie doll collecting community thrives in Europe, so many European-exclusive collector Barbie dolls have appeared over the years. Barbie doll has represented many European retailers such as Burbank Toys, Hamleys, Harvey Nichols, Kastner & Ohler, Pallendorf, Palmers, Spielzeug-Ring, and Vedes with exclusive dolls, and special souvenir Barbie dolls were even created for the Euro Disney and Gardaland theme parks. Austria's Life Ball series of Barbie dolls are the most expensive and desirable dolls created for European collectors; the most recent Life Ball Barbie by designer Valentino wears a replica of the gown Julia Roberts wore to the 2001 Academy Awards ceremony.

Further notable dolls from Europe include those Benetton Barbie dolls not available in the U.S., a collection begun in the early 1990s and revisited in 2005 – 2007. After receiving each of the first few U.S. Happy Holidays Barbie dolls one year after their U.S. debut, Europe offered a unique series of Happy Holidays Barbie dolls of their own in the mid-1990s. One could even make an entire mini-collection simply by purchasing Barbie dolls bearing specific European place names like Ibiza, Milan, Riviera, and St. Tropez.

Europeans were very fond of The Heart Family, friends of Barbie doll sold in the U.S. from 1985 to 1990. Many unique European versions of The Heart Family/La Famille Doucoeur were available, and these dolls and sets have a special section devoted to them. The popularity of The Heart Family toddlers is evidenced by the fact that Mattel Europe produced three different annual series of the children, renamed Barbie Li'l Friends, after The Heart Family franchise was discontinued.

Americans continue to look to Paris for the latest fashion trends, and the latest exclusive Barbie dolls, with the annual release of the Paris Fashion Doll Festival Barbie. The 2006 entry, Rhapsody in Paris Barbie, was limited to only 200 dolls and sent collectors scrambling for the doll. Other recent releases found in this book include the Girls Aloud Fashion Fever collection from England; Girls Aloud is a pop singing group.

European fascination with the royals ensures numerous Princess Collection Barbie and Ken dolls not found in the U.S. Europe, indeed, offers something for every collector.

China

While Mattel's China factory has been masterfully producing Barbie dolls since 1987 for distribution in the U.S. and elsewhere, few Barbie dolls created exclusively for the Chinese market have surfaced. Most notable among the dolls created for China is the ongoing series of Going Home Barbie dolls, available each year since 2002. Created for the White Swan Hotel in Guangzhou, China, Going Home Barbie is a souvenir gift to adopting parents of Chinese children who stay at the hotel. Each Barbie dolls is packaged with an adorable Chinese infant! These dolls are highly prized by the adopting families as well as collectors, making them very valuable.

Hong Kong

Now reunited with mainland China, Hong Kong's primary claim to fame among collectors is the Barbie doll set commemorating Hong Kong's return to Chinese sovereignty in 1997 and the one-year anniversary set released in 1998. Each set features Barbie doll wearing traditional Chinese attire, along with a commemmorative golden token. For the 1998 occasion, the American Mattel CEO Jill Barad wrote, "Since 1959 the Barbie doll has inspired fashion and lifestyle for girls and young ladies everywhere. The popularity of Barbie is truly universal. In her travels around the world, she has influenced renowned international artists and designers to create uniquely distinctive costumes of many different nations...she shows us just how to combine Eastern charm with Western glamour."

India

Collectors took note of India when Barbie in India dolls debuted in 1991. Wearing traditional Indian saris and featuring the Hindu dot on their foreheads, the dolls wore authentic costumes and metal jewelry. More elaborate dolls followed with the Expressions of India collection, and these beauties wore nose rings! Several unique Happy Holidays Barbie dolls were released, but the greatest collector interest remained with the dolls wearing costumes representing the Indian heritage. Indian releases balanced playline dolls like Teacher Barbie, School-Going Skipper, Pretty Hair Barbie, and

numerous unique Kelly dolls with more sophisticated traditional attire like Sundari Gujarati Barbie. An unusual blend of classic Indian detailing with playline appeal is India's Indian Diva Barbie, wearing "ethnic designer wear."

Indonesia

Mattel's Indonesia factory has only been manufacturing Barbie dolls since 1997, and most of those dolls are created for sale in the U.S. and world-wide. Several special commemmorative Indonesian dolls deserve collectors' attention. On the occasion of the first year anniversary of operations, a special Barbie doll exclusive to Indonesia was created in 1998. Then in 2003 a milestone was reached — the Indonesian factory produced one million Barbie dolls in a single week! A special "A Million Thanks" Barbie doll was created to mark that milestone. Another desirable doll created for Indonesia is Minang Barbie, who wears a traditional Indonesian plate-dancer's costume.

Japan

Japan really needs no introduction when it comes to advanced Barbie doll collectors. Mattel's Japanese factory has become synonymous with quality. The vintage 1960s period introduced unique Japanese versions of Midge, Skipper, and Francie dolls. The pink-skinned American Girl Barbie with Lifelike Bendable Legs is a rarity even in Japan, and dressed box versions of Twist 'N Turn Barbie are highly collectible.

Japanese anime influenced the creation of Barbie doll's unique Japanese friend Eli, who has a large head and big eyes. Other anime-inspired dolls of the early 1970s include Tuli-Chan and Cho Cho Chan, anime versions of Francie and Skipper.

While Mattel continued to market dolls that looked like their American counterparts, the Japanese SuperStar Barbie dolls were not appealing to the Japanese children, and an anime-style Barbie doll was created in 1981. This new Barbie doll was more petite than the American version, and she went back to her roots as a 17-year-old high school student. New friends Ellie and Flora joined her and Ken as the unique Japanese world of Barbie doll evolved throughout the 1980s.

Famous Japanese designer Hiromichi Nakano created a collection of American Doll Barbie dolls for sale in Japan; these dolls use the original 1959 Barbie head mold and appealed to the adult collector. Designer Kansai also created a Japanese collection for Barbie, but his doll used the anime-style doll, and the Kansai clothing was marketed to children.

Japan's P.B. Store sold a wonderful collection of dolls for adult collectors. These dolls use the original 1959 Barbie head mold and the 1967 Twist 'N Turn Barbie head mold; some of the dolls wear re-creations of vintage ensembles sold in the U.S., while others wear unique creations.

The anime-look for Barbie doll was mostly abandoned by the early 1990s, although the Japanese Barbie dolls often still had larger eyes than American dolls. Most interesting about Japanese Barbie dolls in the late 1990s is that the Japanese version often uses a different head mold than the exact same doll sold in the U.S.; occasionally the more mature Mackie face would be preferred over the SuperStar face, while in other instances the SuperStar face was used on a Japanese doll when another face was being used on the U.S. doll. Unquestionably, Japan offers a cornucopia of Barbie dolls and styles from which to choose.

Korea

Looking much like the Japanese anime Barbie dolls, the Korean Barbie dolls are overall much rarer than the playline Japanese dolls. Korea introduced two unique Korean friends for Barbie, Danbie and Kotbie, who are rarely found today.

Malaysia

The Kebaya Barbie dolls of Malaysia are the most interesting to collectors. Using the Teresa head mold, these dolls wear traditional Kebaya gowns that are richly adorned.

Philippines

Collectors took note of the Philippines in 1991 when a fantastic series of Filipina Barbie dolls, each limited to only 500 dolls per style, debuted wearing amazingly detailed gowns reflecting the native Filipina style. A second wave of Filipina Barbie dolls appeared in 1993, and only 1,000 dolls per design were offered. While unique playline dolls were offered during the 1980s, it wasn't until the early 1990s that the Philippines began producing almost as many dolls for collectors as for children. The Ethnic Barbie collection featured Barbie doll wearing native costumes from different areas of the Philippines, and the Santacruzan and Flores De Mayo Barbie dolls reflected the deep religious convictions of Filipinos. The Filipino national pride is evident in dolls such as the Centennial Barbie collection of 1998, which commemorated the 100th anniversary of the Philippines' independence. Later collector series like Isla Filipina and Manilena celebrated specific areas around the Philippines, while Fauna Filipina showcased the wildlife found in the Philippines. The playline dolls exclusive to the Philippines are often just as exciting and beautiful to collectors!

Singapore

Singapore made it onto collectors' maps with the release of Singapore Girl Barbie in 1992. Created for Singapore Airlines, the doll uses the Oriental Barbie head mold and was sold in-flight. A second edition Singapore Girl was more widely available. Collectors needed to refer to their maps once again in 2006 with the release of the Singapore exclusive Silkstone Teacher Barbie.

Taiwan

Taiwan is best known to collectors for its series of Haute Couture Barbie dolls of 1992. Several other glamour Barbie dolls were offered exclusively in Taiwan in the early 1990s.

Mexico

Mexico caught collectors' attention in the mid-1970s with the discovery of Barbie doll's unique Mexican friend Valerie. Mexico's versions of Barbie often looked completely different from their American counterparts; the Peinado Magico Barbie of 1975 has the Steffie head with heavy makeup, while her counterpart Quick Curl Barbie in the U.S. has the Twist 'N Turn Barbie head, and their gowns are totally different. Mexico's 1970s themes included Barbie Hawaiiana and Valerie Tahitiana, and Valerie Modello explored a modeling career during the time that SuperStar Barbie had a similar career in the U.S.

The 1980s Mexican dolls also have distinct differences from American dolls. They are more tanned, and their hair is brighter blonde. Entire gimmicks are even eliminated; the Mexico Western Barbie lacks the winking eye feature of the American doll.

Argentina

Rock Star Barbie of Argentina is a lovely variation of her American counterpart, and her band mate is Kenny, not Ken! The gorgeous Argentina Happy Holidays Barbie, Felices Fiestas Barbie, is missing from most Happy Holidays collections.

Brazil

Brazil, the fifth largest nation on earth both in population and in geographic size, is home to some of the most fantastic Barbie dolls ever produced with hair colors, fashions, and themes unique to the Brazilian market. While Mattel's playline Barbie doll was almost always a blonde-haired, blue-eyed incarnation in the U.S. during the 1980s, Brazil's playline Barbie doll was truly a collector's dream with luscious red, brunette, and even platinum white hair colors used on dolls marketed to children! In the U.S. Mattel's Barbie doll used either the SuperStar Barbie body with permanently bent arms or the straight-arms palm-to-rear body, while Brazilian children favored a more pose-able body with arms similar to those used previously by Mattel on the vintage 1970 – 1971 Living Barbie and the 1980 Beauty Secrets Barbie; these arms have embedded wires that permit the elbows to bend, and hands are jointed at the wrists! Mattel cited child safety laws as the reason that these pose-able bodies were discontinued in the U.S., but apparently Brazil had no such mandates since Estrela's Barbie dolls utilized these pose-able arms through 1990.

It might be said that there is no ugly Brazilian Barbie; they all have the same attention to detail.

Estrela's dolls usually sold themselves on the quality of the dolls and fashions alone, ignoring gimmicks to entice young buyers. For Estrela a nondescript night of the gala is all it took to create a fabulous series of costumes for Barbie.

Estrela took some liberties with the names of Barbie doll's acquaintances in Brazil. The most notable name change came with Barbie doll's longtime boyfriend Ken. Apparently Ken is an uncommon name in Brazil, so Estrela renamed him Bob. Bob unceremoniously adopted the name Ken in 1987 but his earlier exploits as a rock performer using the Bob alias are legendary. Midge, Barbie doll's best friend in the U.S., appeared as Viky in Brazil, and Brazilian Debora is Teresa in the U.S. The name changes are just one more reason Estrela's Barbie family dolls are so collectible.

FUN FACTS FOR THE COLLECTOR OF ESTRELA BARBIE DOLLS

*Most of the Estrela Barbie dolls sold from 1984 to 1991 come with a plastic posing stand featuring a large star-shaped base; the star-shaped stand base was created for the 1977 American SuperStar Barbie but was discontinued in the U.S. in 1979. Estrela would naturally continue using this star-shaped posing stand since Estrela literally means "star."

*When found for sale on eBay or sales lists, Estrela dolls are often mistakenly cited as Mexican or Spanish releases, and the language on the box is usually assumed to be Spanish when it is in fact Portugese.

*The SuperStar Ken head mold was used for Estrela's Bob/Ken dolls through 1990, but in the U.S. Mr. Heart of The Heart Family used that head mold exclusively between 1985 and 1990.

*Through 1988 Estrela shrink-wrapped most of their Barbie family dolls.

*Because over half of Brazil's population has Western European ancestry, their Barbie dolls often look more European than Latin.

*Feliz Aniversario Barbie is the Brazilian counterpart to the American Happy Birthday Barbie, and while the two nation's dolls look nothing alike, they do both appear in revised editions several times in the 1980s, each time bringing a boxed gift for the child.

*Collectors prize the metallic vacuumized pumps worn by many of the Estrela female dolls in formal wear.

*Ken's buddy Alan might be thought to have two wives since he married Midge in the U.S. and Viky in Brazil.

*Skipper made her debut in Brazil in 1991 when she served as flower girl at Viky's and Alan's wedding.

*No black Barbie family or friends dolls were produced by Estrela before 1995.

*The number of Brazilian children playing with dolls may be declining, as Brazilian women bore an average of six children in 1960 compared to three children in 2005.

Peru

Peru surprisingly offered some Ken dolls not available in the U.S. Garden Party Ken only appeared in Peru, even though Garden Party Barbie was a playline doll in the U.S. A unique version of SuperStar Barbie sold in Peru also tops many wish lists of collectors of South American dolls.

Venezuela

Llanera Barbie looks like a Venezuelan girl with her cascading brown hair and native costume. Miss Barbie is a Venezuelan beauty queen. Olimpico Ken from Venezuela competed in the 1988 Olympic games; even his head was changed to use the Derek head mold to better reflect a male Venezuelan athlete.

Pricing

Values listed in this book are for NRFB (never removed from box) dolls. This means that the dolls are still perfectly intact and undisturbed inside their original boxes just as they left Mattel's factory. Because many foreign dolls are quite rare, the values are at the discretion of the buyer and seller. Keep in mind that the value of many newer foreign dolls often reflects the high cost of importing the dolls, usually via air mail.

Barbie

Eli

Tuli-Chan

Cho Cho-Chan

Carla

Valerie

Ellie

Flora

Bob

Marina

Laura

Becky

Barbie®

Bibi

Bobby

Noel

Sophie

Stephanie

Danbie

Kotbie

Lia

Viky

Withney

Maoni

Lara

Tina

Debora

Alexia

Marie

Susie/Vicky

Reina

Westley

Shelly

Susie

Julie

Melon/Meron

Peggy

Shelli/Sherri

Cherry

Tamera

Maura

Tabitha

Marina

Foreign Celebrity Friends

Chanta Goya

Wayne Gretzky

Johnny Hallyday

Michael Shumacher

1972 Barbie Fashion Doll #8549, released in 1976, is a rare dressed box doll using the Steffie head mold with straight blonde hair parted on her left, blue eyes, red lips, and pale skin. She wears the 1976 Barbie Best Buys Fashions #9158, a Bicentennial dress featuring a red skirt depicting Revolutionary War soldiers and a blue blouse featuring white lace cuffs and a white lace neckline, along with blue pilgrim shoes. $200.00.

1972 Barbie Fashion Doll #8549, released in 1976, wears a red dress with white lace at the hem, a matching tie-on red jacket with white lace border and sheer red sleeves, and red pilgrim shoes. $200.00.

1972 Barbie Fashion Doll #8549, released in 1977, is a bubble card version of the Australian Gold Medal Barbie. She wears her Olympic costume, a yellow swimsuit with a green collar, and an Olympic gold medal. $125.00.

1972 Barbie Fashion Doll #8549, released in 1977, packages the Stacey-face Malibu Barbie wearing older 1974 – 1976 Barbie Best Buys fashions. The oval gold label on her bubble reads "Barbie FASHION DOLL Twist 'N Turn Waist Bendable Legs c 1972 Mattel Pty. Limited. Melbourne. Printed in Australia." $175.00 each.

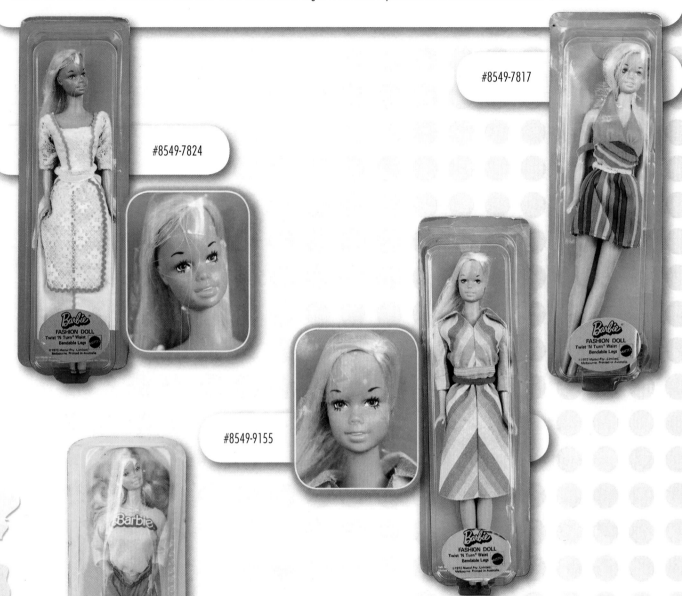

#8549-7817

#8549-7824

#8549-9155

1972 Barbie Fashion Doll #2551, released in 1978, packages SuperStar Barbie wearing the 1978 Barbie Best Buys Fashions #2551, a pink "Barbie" logo shirt with purple shorts, with the addition of white boots. Note that the Melbourne Australia gold label on her bubble now uses the updated "Barbie" name logo. $150.00.

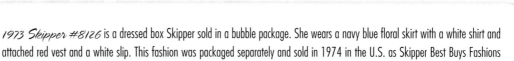

1973 Skipper #8126 is a dressed box Skipper sold in a bubble package. She wears a navy blue floral skirt with a white shirt and attached red vest and a white slip. This fashion was packaged separately and sold in 1974 in the U.S. as Skipper Best Buys Fashions #7773. $325.00.

1989 Gold Coast Barbie #7344 wears a pink and green one-piece swimsuit with black trim. She was made in Malaysia. A very similar doll was sold in Europe as Riviera Barbie, but Riviera Barbie was made in China. $28.00.

1989 The Barbie School Collection #7344 packages Gold Coast Barbie with a blue Barbie thermos. $45.00.

1995 Barbie Fashion Avenue Giftset #0035 packages Fashion Avenue Barbie, wearing Barbie Fashion Avenue fashion #14363, a pink top with an attached yellow skirt accented by white flowers, lacy white leggings, and a pink beret, along with a boxed Barbie Fashion Avenue fashion. $75.00.

1996 *Miss Barbie #61747* wears a red top with a plaid skirt and matching scarf. Red pumps are included. She was manufactured by Richwell Phils for Cole's grocery stores in Australia. $30.00.

1999 *Barbie Exclusive Easter Doll #7585* wears a satiny blue blouse with an attached print purple skirt featuring flowers and rabbits. The blue plastic egg contains cardboard candy, an egg, flowers, a bunny, and a chick, and four real milk chocolate eggs are included. $28.00.

2000 *Barbie Fashion Avenue #23732* is the first of four Australian Collection fashions featuring notable Australian designers. This ensemble, by Jonathan Ward, is a shimmering pink evening gown with attached sheer pink cape, a matching purse, a metallic pink tiara, and metallic-finish pink pumps. $35.00.

2000 *Barbie Fashion Avenue #23729* showcases the talents of Joseph Saba with a pink and orange stretch skirt with a gray coat, a gray purse, and pink shoes. Note that the boxes for these Australian Collection Barbie Fashion Avenues changed during production from 2000 to 2001. $30.00.

2000 Barbie Fashion Avenue #23730 includes MOOKS Clothing Company's denim cuff skirt, red hooded "Mooks" jacket, gray shirt with the MOOKS logo design, a denim handbag with the MOOKS label, and white sneakers. Sally McDonald of MOOKS designed this fashion. $28.00.

2000 Barbie Fashion Avenue #23731 features the talents of Claire Dickson-Smith of Third Millennium with a blue sweater, blue pants, a leopard-print top, a leopard-print hat, a leopard-print handbag, black sunglasses, and black pumps. $30.00.

2000 Barbie Fashion Week #52813 features Barbie doll with a new clothing ensemble for each day of the week. Monday brings a white ice-skating costume with a faux fur-trimmed parka, Tuesday offers a bowling fashion with purple capris and a sleeveless print top, Wednesday features a blue birthday dress, Thursday has a purple shirt with a white skirt featuring purple floral print for shopping, Friday brings a peach gown for a concert with Ken, Saturday calls for a blue dress with black trim for a fashion show, and Sunday means a purple dress for dancing. $65.00.

2001 Barbie Back To School Gift Set #52814 includes Barbie doll with the Generation Girl Barbie head mold wearing a rose top with a pink floral-print skirt and pink open-toe heels. A vinyl pink and purple book bag is included for Barbie, and a large tote, a book, two pencils, a pencil case, an eraser, a pencil sharpener, and a paper clip are included for the child. $50.00.

2001 Barbie Fashion Boutique #52815 includes blue-eyed Barbie and brown-eyed Kelly dolls wearing matching blue sundresses, along with four extra fashions for Barbie doll and three extra fashions for Kelly. $125.00.

2006 The Nurse Barbie #j4253 is an edition of 3,800 Silkstone dolls exclusive to Australia and Europe. Her box states "This nurse is completely committed to her patients — caring and healing every day!" She has brown shoulder-length hair parted on her right, brown eyes, and red lips accentuated by a beauty mark. Her nurse's uniform includes a crisp white belted dress, a matching cap, and a blue cape. White mary janes and pearl earrings complete her look, and a stethoscope, a clipboard, and a pencil are included. $165.00.

Canada

1972 Barbie Fashion Doll #8549, released in 1977, uses the Steffie head mold with pink skin, blue eyes, and straight blonde hair parted on her left. She is in bubble-card packaging wearing one of four Barbie Best Buys fashions sold separately in 1976. The pink sticker on her bubble uses the vintage Barbie signature logo and the 1972 date. $125.00 each.

#8549-9157

#8549-9571

#8549-9575

#8549-9576

Barbie®

1973 Barbie With Twist 'N Turn Waist #8587 wears a yellow version of the 1971 Sun Set Malibu Barbie doll's swimsuit. She uses the Steffie head mold with pale skin and blue eyes, and she uses the Francie arms. The side of her box states "Easy to pose! Long, long hair you can comb!" $95.00.

1973 Twist 'N Turn Barbie #8587, released in 1976, is the same doll as Barbie With Twist 'N Turn Waist, but in a blister card bubble package. Note the new "Barbie" logo on her bubble sticker which indicates she was sold during 1976, when that logo debuted, or later, despite the date printed on the sticker. $75.00.

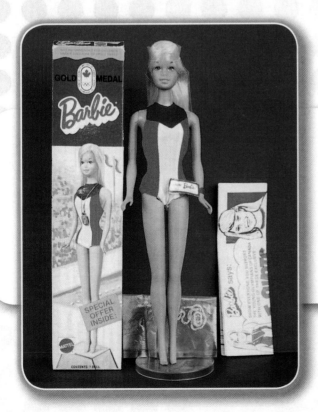

1974 Gold Medal Barbie #7233 wears the same red and white striped swimsuit with blue collar as the U.S. Gold Medal Barbie, but the Canadian doll's gold medal is oval, not round, and features the maple leaf design. The doll from Canada has a wrist tag and uses a bilingual slim photo box with the Olympic rings and the maple leaf motif. A young Olympians of Canada $2.00 t-shirt offer is included. The U.S. doll lacks the wrist tag and has a slim illustrated English-only box with a red, white, and blue shield logo with the Olympic rings. $85.00.

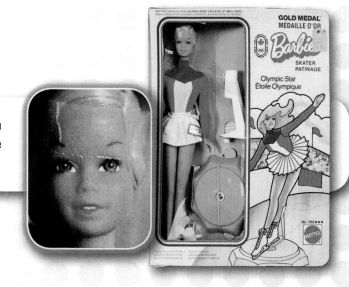

1974 Gold Medal Barbie Skater #7262 is identical to the U.S. version except the Canadian doll wears a wrist tag, and her box features the Canadian maple leaf Olympic logo. $125.00.

1974 Gold Medal Ken 2 Outfits #7475 includes an Olympic ice hockey costume and a number "9" track costume for Ken. $85.00.

1975 Malibu Skipper #1069, released in 1977, wears a yellow and orange swimsuit with a blue collar. $75.00.

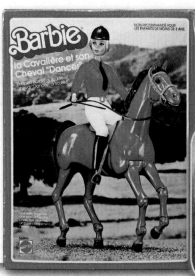

1976 Barbie and Her Horse Dancer #9948 packages poseable Equestrienne Barbie with her poseable horse Dancer. The doll in this set uses the 1967 Twist 'N Turn Barbie head mold with straight blonde hair and bangs, and she has a silver wrist tag featuring a black Mattel logo and her country of origin, Taiwan. $200.00.

1977 Barbie Baby-Sitting Room #7804 is "a happy place where baby is snug 'n safe 'n warm!" This structure was sold in the U.S. as The Sunshine Family Baby's Room, but the room for Barbie has a pink floor and pink walls. The baby's cradle transforms into a buggy, and the starry scene outside the window snaps off for daytime. A rocking chair, a table, a bathtub, a scale, a diaper pail, planters with ferns, two framed pictures, two baby bottles, two jars, a bar of soap, a tray, a rattle, and a blanket are included. The baby packaged with this room is the same Little Sweets doll found in The Sunshine Family Baby's Room although the baby in this set is simply referred to as "Baby." $150.00.

1980 Barbie #7382 is a basic dressed box doll sold on a blister card. These inexpensive dolls wear fashions either sold separately without dolls or worn by previously released dolls. Barbie #7382 uses the Steffie head mold with straight blonde hair and a hollow body with unbending knees. $95.00 each.

1980 Barbie #7382 was released in 1982 using the SuperStar Barbie head mold. These inexpensive dolls wear Barbie Best Buys Fashions sold from 1980 to 1982. $75.00 each.

1982 Angel Face Barbie #5640 is identical to the doll sold in the U.S. except that the Canadian doll was packaged with a free 14-page 1984 Barbie & Ken Mini Calendar. $35.00.

1982 Barbie #5336 is a basic tanned swimsuit Barbie doll using the SuperStar Barbie head mold with blue eyes and straight blonde hair. Each doll has mirrored sunglasses in her hair and wears a basic dress with shoes. $50.00 each.

1983 Playtime Barbie #5336 has unbending smooth plastic legs and wears a red and white striped playsuit with red open-toe heels. $35.00.

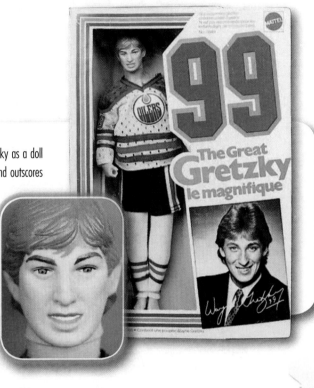

1983 The Great Gretzky #5949 immortalizes Canadian hockey player Wayne Gretzky as a doll with a unique head mold sculpted in his image. The box says "The Great Gretzky outshoots and outscores them all." Gretzky wears the Edmonton Oilers home uniform and comes with a hockey stick, hockey gloves, and ice skates. Born in Ontario in 1961, Gretzky signed with the Edmonton Oilers in 1979 and repeatedly won the Hart Trophy for Most Valuable Player in the NHL. He scored 50 goals in 39 games during the 1981 – 1982 season. He uses the 12" Ken doll body with bent fingers, bendable arms, and a ball-jointed waist; this is the same body used for 1982's All Star Ken. $95.00.

1983 The Great Gretzky Away From Home Uniform #4107 is one of three rare carded costumes created for Wayne Gretzky. $75.00.

1983 The Great Gretzky Jogging Suit #4174. $75.00.

1983 The Great Gretzky Tuxedo #4175. $75.00.

1984 Barbie Dream Carriage With Two Horses #5441 comes with two white horses with black manes. The carriage features three elegant interchangeable door panels, golden carriage lanterns, and moveable carriage wheels. $75.00.

1987 Club California Barbie #4439 and her friends are packaged with a Club California cassette music tape of California songs in French and English. A Club California membership card is also included with each doll in this series. $30.00.

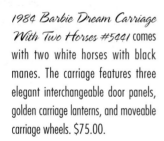

1987 Club California Ken #4441. $30.00.

1987 Club California Midge #4442. $55.00.

1987 Club California Teresa #5503. $55.00.

1987 Club California Christie #4443. $45.00.

1987 Skating Star Barbie #4547 was officially licensed for the Calgary 1988 Olympic Winter Games. Barbie is a beautiful ice princess in her white bodysuit, short skirt with glittery belt, tiara with "jewel," tights, and ice skates. She holds a rose bouquet and comes with a detailed diary chronicling her world travels and competitions. Her diary begins, "Hi! My trip around the world to train and compete as a world-class figure skater is the most exciting thing I've ever done!" $45.00.

1989 Pink Jubilee Barbie is an edition of only 500 dolls in individual round display cases created for Barbie doll's thirtieth anniversary celebration hosted by Mattel Canada on April 11, 1989. Guests received this lovely doll wearing a pink satin gown featuring a jewel on the gathered bodice and a sheer wrap. Her certificate of authenticity states, "This limited edition Pink Jubilee Barbie commemorates the thirty magical years of a very special doll. Designed by Wayne Clark, #— of 500." $500.00.

1990 Fashion Play Barbie #5766 wears the same pink and orange dress as the European version of this doll, but she was made in China and has a much prettier face and a different hairstyle. $25.00.

1992 Woodward's 100 Anniversary Barbie commemorates the 100th anniversary of the Canadian store by pairing Ibiza Barbie with a Barbie Six-Fashion Gift Set. The box sticker proclaims "WOODWARD'S EXCLUSIVE ANNIVERSARY COLLECTION." $50.00.

1993 Enchanted Princess Barbie #10292 is a Sears exclusive sold only in Canada. Barbie wears a lavender skirt with sparkly tulle lavender overskirt and silver lamé sash, a silver lamé bodice accented with a silver star and featuring sparkly sheer lavender sleeves, and a silver star hair decoration. A scepter with ribbon is included. $25.00.

1994 Rollerskating Barbie and Her Roll-Along Puppy #12098 is exclusive to Zellers. Barbie wears a colorful bodysuit, a pink fanny pack, a white jacket, a headband, knee pads, and in-line skates as she walks her white dog, which wears a pink bone and paw-print neck bow. A box of Milkbone dog biscuits, a dog food dish, and a dog magazine are included. $65.00.

1994 Ruffle Fun Barbie #15802 wears a purple minidress featuring pink swirls and yellow dots with a pink ruffle. The U.S. doll wears a pink minidress with a yellow ruffle. $15.00.

1995 Fashion Avenue Barbie #15833 wears a pink top with an attached yellow skirt with flowers at the waist and white lace leggings. A pink beret and pumps complete her ensemble. The fashion she wears was sold as a boxed Fashion Avenue fashion in the U.S. $20.00.

1995 City Style Barbie #10149 commemorates the 325th anniversary of Canada's Hudson's Bay Company, founded in 1670. City Style Barbie wears a white skirt with a matching jacket lined in gold braid over a gold shell and sheer white pantyhose. A white hat with gold band, a white purse on a gold chain, white pumps, a white shopping bag with a gold "B" logo, and a "la Baie" Hudson's Bay shopping bag are included. Only 3,000 dolls were produced. $60.00.

1995 Governor's Ball Barbie #14010 is a second Hudson's Bay exclusive. She wears a metallic green top with gold bow accents over a white satin skirt adorned with gold leaf patterns. A replica of the invitation to the 1967 Governor's Ball, held during Canada's centennial celebration, is included. $45.00.

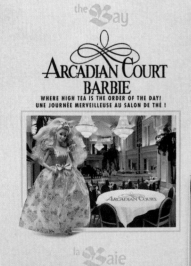

1996 Arcadian Court Barbie #62889 is the third Hudson's Bay exclusive. She is an edition of 2,900 dolls dressed for high tea. Barbie doll wears a white satin dress with a gold-striped bodice and a sheer floral print overskirt. A gold lamé bow adorns her hair, and a short gold lamé bow accents her waist. A doll-size Arcadian Court tablecloth, napkins, and a menu are included. $50.00.

1996 Calvin Klein Jeans Barbie #16211 was sold as a Hudson's Bay exclusive in Canada, although she was sold in the U.S. as a Bloomingdale's exclusive. A sticker on the box front covers the "bloomingdale's LIMITED EDITION" phrase, replacing it with "the Bay la Baie LIMITED EDITION." $32.00.

1996 School Spirit Barbie #63569 wears a black shirt with a double-belted red plaid miniskirt, red leggings, and black boots. A Hudson's Bay striped Point Blanket coat and hat is included for Barbie. $40.00.

1997 Barbie On Bay #63987 wears a pink and white gingham jumper dress with a white t-shirt and a pink hair bow. Also included are a matching cloth purse, a plastic white basket, a white Scottish Terrier dog, and a unique white fleece sweater with pink trim featuring the "Barbie" name on the front and "Barbie on Bay" on the back. $30.00.

1997 Toyland Barbie #64176 wears a pink shirt with a pink and white striped miniskirt, a pink satin jacket, white socks, and pink sneakers. A blue hula hoop, a plush pink teddy bear, and "the Bay" shopping bag are included. $35.00.

1996 Teddy Fun Barbie #15684 wears a white t-shirt featuring a pink bear applique, a white dress featuring a pink bear print, silver hoop earrings, and a denim vest. She carries a pink plush teddy bear. A "ZELLERS" sticker covers the words "Hills Special Edition" on her box front since the doll was a Zellers exclusive in Canada but a Hills exclusive in the U.S. $20.00.

1997 Barbie Loves Zellers #19020 wears a pink sweater with a pastel print collar, cuffs, and matching headband and a denim miniskirt with a white belt. She carries a "Barbie <heart> Zellers" shopping bag. $20.00.

1997 Daniel Hechter Barbie #18984 was created for the Fairweather store. She wears a red DH SPORT top, black leggings, and white sneakers. She carries black sunglasses and comes with a black DH SPORT nylon tote bag. $28.00.

1999 Barbie Outdoor Beauty Store includes Riviera Barbie wearing a blue sundress with white daisy designs and blue open-toe heels with her plastic store kiosk with awning. The box liner states "Barbie sells the best products!" A cash register, plastic beauty products, and shopping bags are included. $35.00.

2000 Cherokee Style Barbie #27991 uses the Generation Girl Barbie head mold with brown eyes. She wears an ankle-length Cherokee-label skirt, a cream-colored top with a maroon vest, and brown boots. She carries a Cherokee portfolio containing a first-place ribbon and a report card indicating she earned an A+ in math, English, science, and history. $25.00.

2000 Fashion Doll Gift Set #27625 packages the U.S. FTD Florists My Special Things Bouquet Barbie wearing her pink sundress with white floral designs inside the FTD Florists purple and pink resin purse vase; this doll and vase were originally sold in the U.S. with a bouquet of real flowers for $59.99, but this Canadian set offers the vase as a school supplies holder. A pencil, stickers, and crayons are included. Strangely, Barbie doll still carries her cardboard FTD basket that states, "Enjoy the flowers! Love, Barbie." $35.00.

2000 Tommy & Kelly Love To Learn With Teacher Barbie #28371 includes Teacher Barbie with the Generation Girl Barbie head mold wearing a blue dress with a black school icons print vest, student Kelly with blue eyes wearing a denim jumper over a red t-shirt with shoes, and student Tommy with rooted golden blond hair wearing a blue shirt, jeans, and sneakers. Two red and black student desks, a black board with clock featuring five school sounds, chalk, and school supplies are included. $85.00.

2000 Halloween Shelly #50533 has white hair and wears a silver lamé space suit with an alien headband. The Halloween Party Kelly sold in the U.S. wearing this costume has purple hair. $45.00.

2001 Coca-Cola Fun Barbie #52717 is dressed for skateboarding in her red Coca-Cola t-shirt, denim shorts, red helmet, red arm and knee pads, and sneakers. She carries a bottle of Coca-Cola and comes with a red Coca-Cola logo skateboard. $30.00.

2002 Coca-Cola Noel Barbie wears a sparkly red shirt with a silver snowflake design, white pants with red bubbles and the Coca-Cola design, and red boots. She holds a Coca-Cola bottle tied with a red ribbon and comes with three cardboard holiday ornaments. $30.00.

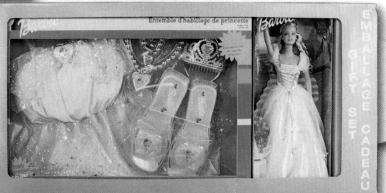

2002 Barbie Outdoor Beauty Store Special Value! #0240 packages the Barbie Outdoor Beauty Store #B0240 with Spring Barbie #B0972. $35.00.

2002 Princess Barbie Gift Set packages Princess Barbie wearing a pink princess gown and a tiara with the child's Barbie Princess Dress-Up Set. $35.00.

2003 Barbie Gift Set #c1407 packages Boutique Barbie with three carded Barbie fashions and the Barbie Kitchen Playset. The doll, fashions, and playset were all available separately at most stores. $45.00.

2003 Chick Marina #61801 has the "toon look" large head with brown hair and green eyes. She wears a yellow chick costume with orange leggings and a purple plastic "shell" that can be decorated with stickers. She is identical to the Easter Tweets Maria sold in the U.S. $20.00.

2003 Sears 50 Barbie #c2699 commemorates the 50th anniversary of Sears in Canada. Barbie doll wears a floral print satin lavender dress, and she carries a lavender purse. The box front has a golden "Sears 50" with the words "Quality, Value, Service, Trust." $20.00.

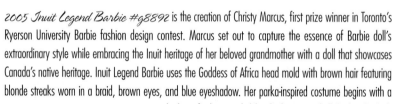

2005 Inuit Legend Barbie #g8892 is the creation of Christy Marcus, first prize winner in Toronto's Ryerson University Barbie fashion design contest. Marcus set out to capture the essence of Barbie doll's extraordinary style while embracing the Inuit heritage of her beloved grandmother with a doll that showcases Canada's native heritage. Inuit Legend Barbie uses the Goddess of Africa head mold with brown hair featuring blonde streaks worn in a braid, brown eyes, and blue eyeshadow. Her parka-inspired costume begins with a bodice of white sueded brushed tricot embellished with plush trim and ribbon and cord accents. The skirt of printed sueded tricot features plush trim with vibrant printed skirt panels reminiscent of the Inuit prints and is worn with a brown satin underskirt. Accessories include gloves, boots, and a cord and feather choker. Only 5,000 dolls were produced. $95.00.

2006 French Maid Barbie #j0966 is an edition of 5,200 Silkstone dolls. Her box states "No mere career girl, this tres belle domestic diva has everything in its stylish place!" She uses the vintage 1959 Barbie head mold with blonde hair parted on her left and worn in an updo hairstyle. A beauty mark accents her red lips. Her uniform includes a crisp black dress accented with white cuffs and a white collar, a white apron, and a white petticoat. A white cap and alluring black fishnet stockings lend an air of sophistication. Black mary janes and a feather duster complete her ensemble. $85.00.

2006 Glamorous Barbie is the souvenir doll from Mattel Canada's first sponsored national Barbie convention, held September 21 – 23, 2006, in Alberta. Christy Marcus, the Canadian designer of Inuit Barbie, designed Glamorous Barbie doll's gown — a brilliant red dress with shimmering red lining, a red tulle train, and a lovely red shawl. Glamorous Barbie has the vintage 1959 Barbie head mold with blonde hair and curly bangs, blue eyes, and red lips. A single flower adorns her updo hairstyle, and she wears pearl earrings, a pearl necklace, and black pumps. An individually numbered sketch signed by Christy Marcus, a metal convention pin depicting the doll, and a doll stand are included. Her wrist tag reads "BARBIE COLLECTORS CLUB OF ALBERTA" on the front and "Glamorous Sept. 21, 22, 23 2006 Christy Marcus" on the back. The label on the interior of her box liner beneath her feet reads "EXCLUSIVE TO CANADIAN NATIONAL CONVENTION Glamorous Sept. 21, 22, 23 2006." Only 349 dolls were produced. $300.00.

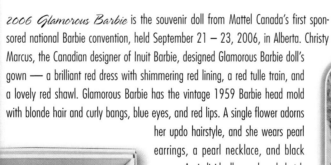

1964 Bubblecut Barbie #850 (Germany) has the Bubblecut hairstyle of the U.S. version, but in Germany some dolls wore the gold and white swimsuit of Fashion Queen Barbie. $450.00.

1964 Swirl Ponytail Barbie #850 (Germany) is found in the U.S. wearing a one-piece red helenca swimsuit, but in Germany the doll was dressed in the gold and white Fashion Queen Barbie swimsuit. $575.00.

1966 Barbie with "Lifelike" Bendable Legs #1163 (Germany) uses the Twist 'N Turn Barbie head mold minus the rooted eyelashes. She has pink skin, blue eyes that glance to her right, rosy cheeks, and red lips. A blue hair ribbon accents her straight hair with bangs, and she wears the one-piece swimsuit with striped pink bodice and attached blue shorts of the American edition. The American version uses the original 1959 Barbie head mold with short hair and bangs. $1,600.00.

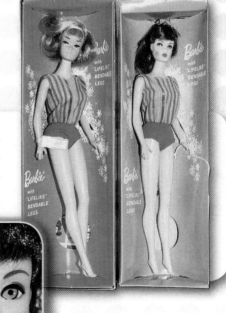

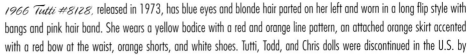

1966 Tutti #8128, released in 1973, has blue eyes and blonde hair parted on her left and worn in a long flip style with bangs and pink hair band. She wears a yellow bodice with a red and orange line pattern, an attached orange skirt accented with a red bow at the waist, orange shorts, and white shoes. Tutti, Todd, and Chris dolls were discontinued in the U.S. by 1971 due to the wires in their bodies not meeting new U.S. safety laws, but the three friends reappeared in Europe several years later. These European exclusive dolls are Japanese-made and use the 1966-dated shrink-wrapped boxes with stickers that say "MADE IN JAPAN," and they have the larger, softer Japanese heads, unlike the smaller, hard Hong Kong heads that debuted with the 1973-dated window boxes. $250.00.

1966 Tutti #8128, released in 1973, has blue eyes and brown hair parted on her left and worn in a long flip style with bangs and a pink hair band. She wears a yellow bodice with a red and orange line pattern, an attached yellow skirt accented with a red bow at the waist, yellow shorts, and white shoes. $250.00.

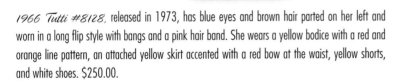

1966 Todd #3590, released in 1973, has titian hair and wears a blue shirt, red and blue plaid shorts, a red cap, white socks, and red shoes. In contrast, the original 1967 Todd wore white, blue, and red checked shorts with a matching checked cap. $200.00.

1966 Chris #8130, released in 1973, has either blonde or brown straight hair worn with a part on her left side and with bangs. A green metal barrette and two green satin bows adorn her hear. This rare European edition wears a horizontally striped red, white, and blue dress with vertically striped matching shorts and red shoes. $425.00.

1967 Talking Stacey #1125 is identical to the Talking Stacey sold in the U.S., but her box has some differences. The box lid is labeled "ROSEBUD MATTEL" to indicate Mattel's England licensee, and the box style is completely different from both the original slim plastic box and cardboard box used in the U.S. Most interestingly, the American boxes identify Stacey as "BARBIE'S BRITISH FRIEND," while in England Stacey is simply "BARBIE'S FRIEND." She debuts the Stacey head mold, and she has bangs and a side ponytail tied with a green satin ribbon, and she wears a diagonally striped two-piece swimsuit. $475.00.

1972 New Beautiful Francie #8520 (Germany) debuts a new look for Barbie doll's cousin Francie. She has a large head with big blue eyes and long blonde hair parted on her left and the straight-legs Francie body. She wears a brown dress with a white collar, white knee socks, and brown shoes. $2,200.00.

1972 Twist and Pose Barbie (England) uses the Stacey head mold with pale skin, blonde hair parted on her left, and blue eyes with painted eyelashes. The sticker on her bubble package features an offer for a 1972 Barbie fashion. $200.00.

1972 Twist 'N Turn Barbie #8587 (Italy) uses the Stacey head mold with pale skin, titian red hair parted on her left, and blue eyes with painted eyelashes. She wears the same one-piece blue swimsuit as the Sun Set Malibu Barbie. $250.00.

1972 Barbie with Bendable Legs #8588 uses the 1967 Twist 'N Turn Barbie head mold with pale pink skin, straight blonde hair parted on her left and worn in two banded sections, and centered blue eyes with painted eyelashes. She wears a hot pink one-piece swimsuit. The earliest version of this doll on the market has a Genuine Barbie wrist tag and is packaged in bubble card packaging. $250.00.

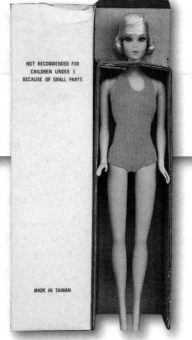

1973 Barbie with Bendable Legs #8588 (England) appeared in England in a purple cardboard box minus the wrist tag. The sides and back of the box feature illustrations of this doll, and her box states "Easy to pose! Long, long hair you can comb!" $315.00.

1973 Barbie with Bendable Legs #8588 has also been found in a white mailer box. $175.00.

1972 Quick Curl Francie Special Offer!! #4222 (England) is identical to the American doll except for the sticker on her package window that features a "½ PRICE COSTUME OFFER." $175.00.

1972 Barbie Christmas Gift Set (England) is exclusive to the United Kingdom's Burbank Toys. This special set packages Quick Curl Barbie with an extra carded Barbie Best Buys fashion. The artwork on the package depicts Barbie doll with gray hair, gray eyes, and pink skin. The box back states "Barbie is the world's most famous fashion model. She loves to be the first to wear the latest clothes and fashion accessories." This historic set marks the first time that the word "Christmas" is found on a Barbie doll's box front. $225.00 each style.

1972 Twist 'N Turn Skipper #8519 wears a swimsuit featuring a white floral print on blue top accented by a single white bow and an attached pleated white skirt. $650.00.

1973 Barbie's Sweet 16 #7796 (Germany) is identical to the U.S. set except for the German sticker. Barbie doll wears a pink dress with white polka dots and white shoes for her sixteenth birthday, and a ribbed yellow "SWEET 16" tank top and blue denim cut-off shorts are a special birthday outfit. $150.00.

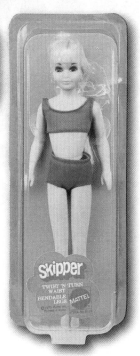

1973 Twist 'N Turn Skipper #8126 has pale skin, straight light blonde hair with bangs, and she wears a two-piece blue swimsuit. She was sold packaged on blister card bubble packaging or inside an orange box. $275.00 each.

Barbie 49

1973 Tutti #8128 has straight blonde hair with bangs worn with a pink hair ribbon. She wears a pink bodice with an attached white skirt featuring a blue floral pattern, and a yellow bow or a blue bow accents her waist. She wears attached shorts that match her skirt, and white shoes, and a tiny pink comb and brush are included. Her 1973 dated box has illustrations of Tutti, Todd, and Chris on the back. $100.00.

1973 Todd #8129 has titian hair and brown eyes. He wears a blue shirt, red shorts, and a red cap. He comes with white socks and white shoes. $95.00.

1973 Todd #8129 (England) was released in England wearing blue and white horizontally striped shorts, a blue shirt, a red cap, white socks, and white shoes. $185.00.

1973 Chris #8130 has brown eyes and reddish brown hair worn with a green barrette and two green hair bows. She wears a yellow dress with green and pink flowers, panties, and white shoes. $125.00.

1974 Carla #8130 is "Tutti's friend," the only black child in Barbie doll's world until the African-American Heart Family twins debuted in 1985. Carla has black hair worn with bangs and pigtails tied with ribbons. She wears an orange dress with white pockets, lacy white collar and waistband, white panties, white socks, and white shoes. $100.00.

1974 Tutti Night-Night, Sleep Tight #7455 packages Tutti with blonde hair and bangs with a pink hair band wearing a lime green nightgown with white lace at the hem, a white lace-trimmed robe, and white slippers. Her box suggests "Dress her for bed, then put her to sleep on her very own bed. Cover her with her bedspread." This is one of three sets made in Hong Kong for sale in Europe. Each set includes a tiny pink comb and brush. $275.00.

1974 Tutti Swing-a-Ling #7453 features blonde Tutti with an orange hair band wearing a yellow bodice with orange sleeves, an orange skirt with yellow trim, white panties, white socks, and orange shoes as she swings on her swing set. Her box advises "Change Tutti's pretty dress! Swing her on her very own swing." $300.00.

1974 Tutti Walkin' My Dolly #7454 includes blonde, blue-eyed Tutti wearing a red and white gingham dress with white lace trim, a pink satin hair band, a white hat, and red shoes. She pushes a red and white doll carriage holding an unpainted baby doll with a blanket. Her box back suggests "Change Tutti's clothes. Wheels turn and hood moves on carriage. Remove baby bunting and play with baby." $300.00.

1974 Barbie Hair Fair #4044 is a European reissue of the 1971 Barbie Hair Fair set sold in the U.S. The new set is almost identical to the original but the European head has painted, not rooted, eyelashes. $125.00.

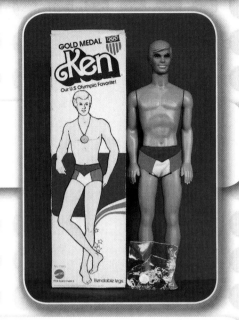

1974 Gold Medal Ken #7380 is a Malibu Ken wearing a red, white, and blue bikini swimsuit. He is packaged in a slim illustrated box with a gold medal. $75.00.

1974 Funtime Barbie #7192 has blonde side-parted hair worn in two rubber banded sections. She uses the Twist 'N Turn Barbie head mold with painted eyelashes and centered blue eyes. She wears a one-piece orange swimsuit. Unlike the darkly suntanned Malibu dolls sold in the U.S., the Caucasian Funtime dolls of Europe have very pale skin tones. $95.00.

1974 Funtime Cara #7185 (Italy) uses the original 1968 Talking Christie head mold with straight black hair. She wears a red one-piece swimsuit with sunglasses. She is identical to the 1973 Malibu Christie sold in the U.S., but in Italy she was called Funtime Cara. $325.00.

1974 Funtime Ken #7194 uses the 1969 Talking Ken head mold with dark brown hair, blue eyes, and pale skin. He wears blue swim trunks. $85.00.

1974 Malibu Ken #1088 has been found in the European Funtime Ken box. The boxes for Malibu Ken and Funtime Ken are very similar, and both dolls share the same head mold and wear swim trunks, so a factory mix-up is understandable. $65.00.

1974 Funtime Skipper #7193 has a pale skin tone and wears a yellow two-piece swimsuit. $95.00.

1976 Funtime Skooter #7381 uses the original 1964 Skipper head mold with auburn hair worn in a side-part flip hairstyle with bangs and blue eyes. She has pale skin and wears a two-piece blue swimsuit. $275.00.

1975 Barbie Moveable Arms & Legs! #7382 wears a hot pink one-piece swimsuit. She uses the 1967 Twist 'N Turn Barbie head mold with hair parted on her left and worn in two banded sections. She has pale skin and unbending straight legs. $95.00.

1975 Barbie Moveable Arms & Legs! #7382 was reissued with the Steffie head mold and straight hair parted on her left. $65.00.

1975 Deluxe Quick Curl Skipper #9428 has pale skin, freckles, and a side-part flip hairstyle. She wears a pink dress with a white fringed stole, a white pearl necklace, and pink flats. A blonde fall hairpiece with attached pink ribbon and hair styling accessories are included. $115.00.

1976 Beautiful Bride Barbie #9907 is actually SuperStar Barbie dressed in an ivory lace wedding gown with a white headband and tulle veil, white ankle strap shoes, and the SuperStar rhinestone earrings, necklace, and hand ring. She carries a bouquet of plastic flowers tied by a satin ribbon. A white version of the pink SuperStar Barbie posing stand is included. $125.00.

1976 *Tutti #8128* has blonde hair with bangs and blue eyes that glance to her right. She wears a yellow dress with white lace trim around the collar and at the hem, white panties, a pink headband, white socks, and white shoes. $85.00.

1976 *Todd #8129* has brown hair and brown eyes. He wears a red shirt with a plaid collar, blue shorts, white socks, and blue shoes. $75.00.

1976 *Chris #8130* has two pink ribbons and a barrette in her brown hair. She wears a blue dress with a central white panel featuring yellow trim, white panties, white socks, and yellow shoes. $95.00.

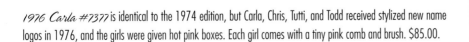

1976 *Carla #7377* is identical to the 1974 edition, but Carla, Chris, Tutti, and Todd received stylized new name logos in 1976, and the girls were given hot pink boxes. Each girl comes with a tiny pink comb and brush. $85.00.

1976 Tutti Night-night, Sleep Tight #7455 is virtually identical to the 1974 set except the box is now hot pink and features the stylized new Tutti logo. $250.00.

1976 Tutti Walkin' My Dolly #7454 is virtually identical to the 1974 set except the box is now hot pink and features the stylized new Tutti logo. $275.00.

1976 Barbie Moveable Arms & Legs! #7382 uses the Stacey head mold with pale skin. She wears a blue bikini. $150.00 each.

1976 Tempo Libero Barbie #9900 (Italy) uses the 1967 Twist 'N Turn Barbie head mold with straight blonde hair and bangs. She has busy hands and wears the Equestrienne Barbie fashion. This Italian doll has a silver Mattel wrist tag on her right wrist. $150.00.

Equestrienne Barbie

1976 Equestrienne Barbie #9900 wears a red-orange bodysuit with a black necktie, cream riding pants with a belt, and black boots. A black hat, an English saddle, and a riding crop are included. She has the 1967 Twist 'N Turn Barbie head mold with eyes that glance to her right, painted eyelashes, and straight blonde hair with bangs. She utilizes the Living Barbie body with bendable arms, jointed wrists, and busy hands so that she can realistically sit on a horse and hold the reins. $125.00.

Equestrienne Barbie

1976 Equestrienne Barbie #9900, released in 1978, received the SuperStar Barbie head mold with centered eyes and side-parted hair with bangs in 1978. The doll's costume and accessories are identical to the 1976 edition but she is harder to find. $145.00.

1976 Dancer #7385 is Barbie doll's poseable brown horse with black mane and tail. Dancer first appeared in the U.S. in 1971 and was reissued in Europe in 1976. An English side saddle, bridle, reins, and bit are included for proper European riding. $50.00.

1976 *Partytime Barbie #9925* uses the Twist 'N Turn Barbie head mold with side-parted blonde hair worn in two pigtails, blue eyes, and rooted and painted eyelashes. She wears a party dress featuring a gold lamé top, a coral skirt with a gold net overskirt, and coral ankle strap shoes. $175.00.

1976 *Partytime Barbie #9925* (France) uses the Steffie head mold with rooted eyelashes and side-parted straight hair in France. Her gold lamé bodice has silvered. $150.00.

1976 *Partytime Barbie #9925* (France) debuts a new party dress featuring a gathered red bodice, a black floral print skirt, and ankle strap shoes. Despite the costume change, her box illustration featuring the original Partytime ensemble remained unchanged. She has the Steffie head mold with rooted eyelashes and side-parted straight hair. $125.00.

1976 *Partytime Barbie #9925* received another revision before being discontinued. She was released with the SuperStar Barbie head mold with side-parted blonde hair, blue eyes, and rooted and painted eyelashes. This is the *only* use of rooted eyelashes on the SuperStar Barbie head mold until 1992, when the Classique Benefit Ball Barbie appeared. $135.00.

1976 Partytime Ken #9927 wears a black tuxedo featuring a pink shirt with a black bow tie and ruffles, attached cummerbund, and black shoes. He uses the 1969 Talking Ken head mold with brown hair and blue eyes. $100.00.

1976 Partytime Skipper #9926 has painted and rooted eyelashes and straight blonde hair with bangs. She wears a yellow party dress with a satin bodice and sheer lace trimmed overskirts and yellow flats. $100.00.

1976 Simpatia Skipper #7379 (Italy) wears a yellow and orange swimsuit with a blue collar. $65.00.

1976 Sporting Barbie #9949 (Italy) is "the girl of the '70's who loves active sports!" She uses the 1967 Twist 'N Turn Barbie head mold with side-glancing blue eyes and straight blonde hair with bangs. She uses the poseable 1969 Living Barbie body with busy hands. She wears a tennis fashion consisting of a yellow satin bodysuit with a white skirt accented by four yellow buttons. Denim riding pants with an attached metallic silver belt and riding boots can be worn with her bodysuit for horse riding. Tennis shoes, a tennis racket, a tennis ball, a saddle, and a riding crop are included. She is very rare. $350.00.

1976 Superstar Barbie #9720 (Germany) is essentially a dressed box version of SuperStar Barbie since the original SuperStar Barbie with sun streaked blonde hair held in place with a Mattel string through her head is packaged wearing fashions sold separately in the U.S. Each doll wears the original rhinestone SuperStar Barbie necklace, earrings, and hand ring. The doll shown here wears the Barbie Get-Ups 'N Go "Flowery Delight Is Party Right!" #2302 fashion, a yellow gown with sheer yellow floral print overskirt and matching sheer shawl. She holds a coral purse, and ankle strap SuperStar shoes are included with each SuperStar Barbie doll. $250.00.

1976 Superstar Barbie #9720 (Germany) is shown here wearing the Get-Ups 'N Go "Lady in Blue, a Romantic View!" fashion #2303 featuring a satin blue bodice with sheer white sleeves, a blue skirt with tiers of sheer white panels, a white satin waist bow, and a white hat with blue satin ribbon. $250.00.

1976 Superstar Barbie #9720 (Germany) wears Mattel's Marie Osmond's "Peasant Sensation" Deluxe TV Fashions #2492 featuring a pink blouse with sheer pink sleeves, a black skirt decorated with pink floral print and accented with a pink ruffle at the hem, and a matching shawl. The green vest and microphone originally included with Marie's fashion are omitted for this doll. $265.00.

1976 Superstar Barbie #9720 (Germany) wears Barbie Best Buys fashion #2229, a multicolored striped skirt worn with a matching vest and a yellow blouse. $250.00.

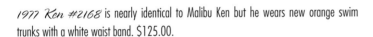

1977 Barbie #2166 uses the Stacey head mold with suntanned skin, painted eyelashes, and straight blonde hair parted on her left. She wears a pink, orange, coral, and white one-piece swimsuit. $140.00.

1977 Ken #2168 is nearly identical to Malibu Ken but he wears new orange swim trunks with a white waist band. $125.00.

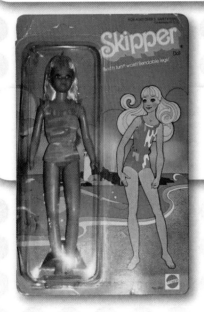

1977 Skipper #2167 is nearly identical to Malibu Skipper but she wears a new pink, orange, coral, and white one-piece swimsuit. $150.00.

1978 Barbie Hair Happening #2267 includes a SuperStar Barbie head with short side-parted silky blonde hair and blue eyes. The set boasts, "Quick change hair fashions for daytime or date time!" and includes a brown wig, a blonde wig, a blonde fall with satin ribbon, an orange hat, a yellow satin ribbon, a brush, and a comb. $75.00.

1978 Beach Fun Barbie #2681 wears a blue, yellow, and orange one-piece swimsuit. She carries a yellow beach bag featuring a decal of the Barbie logo inside a star. She has the SuperStar Barbie head mold with tan skin. $65.00.

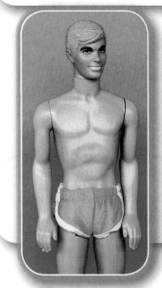

1978 Beach Fun Ken #2683 wears orange swim trunks with the "K" logo. He comes with a "Ken" logo tote bag. $65.00.

1978 Beach Fun Skipper #2682 is a Malibu Skipper wearing a yellow, blue, and orange one-piece swimsuit. She carries a yellow beach tote featuring a decal of the Skipper logo inside a star. $75.00.

1978 Hawaiian Superstar Barbie #2289 features SuperStar Barbie with black side-part hair, brown eyes, and blue eyeshadow. She wears an orange floral print bikini with a long matching tie-on skirt and a green floral lei with pink flowers. A green "grass" skirt, a windsurfer with sail, and a ukulele are included. $500.00.

1978 Picture Pretty Barbie #2290 packages SuperStar Barbie wearing a shiny gold bodice and a yellow skirt with sheer yellow overskirt and yellow ankle strap SuperStar shoes with an orange camera and an orange spotlight. $500.00.

1979 Barbie Sun #1067 (Spain) uses the SuperStar Barbie head mold. She has tan skin with painted-on tan lines under her aqua bikini, and she wears mirrored sunglasses. $75.00.

1979 Barbie Sun Acapulco Fashion #20041 (Spain) is a blue jumpsuit with a blue scarf and blue ankle strap shoes. $95.00.

1979 Ebony Christie #1293 uses the Steffie head mold with a black afro hairstyle, brown skin, and brown eyes. She wears a sparkly red bodysuit featuring gold trim at the neckline, red earrings, a sparkly red skirt, and red ankle strap shoes. She is identical to the historic Black Barbie, the first African-American Barbie doll, but in Europe she was simply Ebony Christie, a friend of Barbie. $125.00.

1979 Black Barbie #1293 is shown here for comparison to Ebony Christie. $75.00.

1979 Jeans Barbie #3901 wears denim jeans, a sparkly red tank top, and shoes. $40.00.

1979 Jeans Skipper #3902 wears a rust colored shirt with jeans and white sneakers. $55.00.

1979 Princess Barbie #1039 wears a tiered white gown, a red sash with "medals," a thin golden crown, a necklace with a single sequin, and white ankle strap shoes. A golden scepter is included. Princess Barbie is very similar to the U.S. Royal Barbie from the International/Dolls of the World collection but her face is redder, her makeup is different, and the color of the sequins on her necklace and sash are different. Her box front says, "She's a royal beauty!" $120.00.

1979 Sports Star Barbie #1334 wears a tennis costume featuring an orange bodice with white stripe and blue border, and a pleated white skirt. Sneakers, a tennis racket, and a tennis racket cover are included. $40.00.

1979 Sports Star Ken #1336 wears white shorts, a white shirt with orange and blue trim, and white sneakers. He comes with a tennis racket and a tennis racket cover. $45.00.

1979 Sports Star Skipper #1335 wears an orange top with blue trim and an attached pleated white skirt. White sneakers, a tennis racket, and a tennis racket cover are included. $50.00.

1979 Chantal Goya #8935-63 (France) has a head mold sculpted in the popular French singer's likeness. Chantal wears a wine colored, floral print dress with lacy white collar. She comes with white socks, red clogs with ankle straps, a white star-shaped posing stand, and a microphone. The box identifies Chantal Goya as "the most popular singer among children." $100.00.

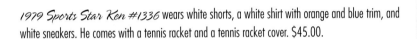

1979 *Chantal Goya* #8935-63 (France) was also sold wearing her Sarouel fashion #8936. The box, stock number, and photos are identical on both Chantal Goya boxes, so the Sarouel dress was likely substituted near the end of production when the supply of Chantal's signature wine colored dress was depleted. $85.00.

1979 *Chantal Goya Fashions* (France) are four ensembles that range from casual to dressy. On the box back Chantal writes, "I have chosen these 4 fashions from my wardrobe for you." $100.00 each.

#8938 *Campagne*.

#8937 *Romantique*.

#8936 *Sarouel*.

#8939 *Week-end*.

1980 Barbie Designer Originals #8233 (France) includes a pink t-shirt featuring the "Chantal Goya" logo, cuffed jeans, and red cork wedgies. $75.00.

1980 Disco Barbie #3207 wears a sparkly golden sleeveless top with a metallic gold waistband and attached white shorts trimmed in gold. Yellow sunglasses, a metallic gold purse, and open-toe heels are perfect for a night out dancing. In Canada, the Disco dolls were called "Golden Nights" and had "Golden Nights" stickers over the word "Disco" on their boxes. $50.00.

1980 Disco Ken #3208 wears white pants with an attached brown shirt, a golden waist band with gold suspenders, a metallic gold bowtie, and white shoes. $60.00.

1980 Disco Skipper #3209 wears a sparkly golden sleeveless top with attached white shorts and a golden waistband, and she comes with yellow sunglasses, a gold purse, and shoes. $55.00.

1980 Golden Dream Barbie #1874 (France) uses the SuperStar Barbie head mold with a pinker skin tone and completely different facial paint than the version sold in the U.S. and elsewhere. Her gold bodysuit, pants, and gloves are also a dull gold color, while her costume is a much brighter, shiny gold on the U.S. doll. $65.00.

The U.S. Golden Dream Barbie close-up is shown for comparison the French version.

1980 My First Barbie #1875 (England) is the first poseable Barbie doll designed for younger children with her smooth bendable legs and special clothing for easy dressing. The American My First Barbie has *non-bending* smooth legs. This edition from England wears a one-piece yellow dress with a red waist tie and red open-toe heels. She is packaged with a 40-page "World of Barbie Handbook" which reveals that in 1981 only 10 different Barbie dolls were offered for sale in the U.K., not counting Ken and Skipper, and recommends the dolls for girls between 4 – 13 years old (this is several years later than girls today admit to playing with Barbie). $50.00.

1980 My First Barbie #1875 (Germany) wears a one-piece blue floral print dress featuring white lapels and a red waist tie. A My First Barbie Handbook is included. $50.00.

1980 My First Barbie #1875 (Germany) wears a yellow swimsuit with blue trim, yellow pants, and a pink hairbow. She is packaged with a striped halter top and a blue skirt that mix and match with her yellow fashion pieces. An additional carded My First Barbie Fashions outfit is attached to her box. $60.00.

1980 Western Barbie #3469 uses the SuperStar Barbie head without the winking-eye mechanism, but she has the busy hands featuring jointed thumbs that allow her to hold her horse's reins. $65.00.

1981 Barbie Et Son Chien Prince #655 (France) packages either Hispanic Barbie or Pretty Changes Barbie with Prince, Barbie doll's afghan dog. $135.00.

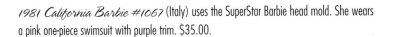

1981 California Barbie #1067 (Italy) uses the SuperStar Barbie head mold. She wears a pink one-piece swimsuit with purple trim. $35.00.

1981 *Feliz Cumpleaños Barbie #1922* (Spain) has platinum hair and pink skin. She wears a white party dress featuring a blue and pink tiered lacy bodice and a layered skirt. The American Happy Birthday Barbie has tan skin and darker blonde hair, and the bodice on her dress is not as colorful. $65.00.

1981 *Jogging Barbie #3986* wears a white and yellow tank top with the number "102," purple shorts, and white sneakers. $35.00.

1981 *Jogging Ken #3988* wears a white and yellow tank top with blue trim featuring the number "103," purple shorts, and white sneakers. $40.00.

1981 *Jogging Skipper #3987* wears a white and yellow tank top with blue trim featuring the number "101," purple shorts, and white sneakers. $40.00.

1981 *Princesa Barbie #1039* (Spain) wears a tiered white gown, a red sash with "medals," a shiny hard plastic crown, a necklace with a sequin, and white ankle strap shoes. A golden scepter is included. Princesa Barbie is very similar to the American Royal Barbie and the European Princess Barbie but her gown lacks the sequined collar found on their dresses, Princesa Barbie doll's skin tone and makeup are darker, and the medals on her red sash differ. $145.00.

1981 *Snoprinsessa Barbie #5359* wears a faux-fur trimmed parka with white cloth boots. The same fashion is worn by the American Eskimo Barbie, but Snoprinsessa Barbie doll uses the SuperStar Barbie head mold with pale skin and blue eyes, while Eskimo Barbie has the Oriental Barbie head mold with tan skin and brown eyes. $250.00.

1981 *Barbie Designer Originals #5150* is the same parka with boots worn by Snoprinsessa Barbie doll. This fashion was sold in those European countries that did not offer the rare Snoprinsessa Barbie, and the fashion is unique to Europe since the U.S. offered the fashion on Eskimo Barbie. $50.00.

1981 Snoprinsessa Barbie Hundeslede #5408 is a brown plastic sled pulled by two Siberian Husky dogs. A furry blanket is included. $225.00.

1981 Superstar Barbie Atardecer #14031 (Spain) wears a white sundress with a red neck-band, a white coat with red trim, and a white hat. $300.00.

1981 Superstar Barbie Casino #22521 (Spain) wears a white gown with a silver collar and waistband and a sheer coat featuring gold accents for a dramatic look. This costume is similar in style to the 1978 boxed SuperStar Barbie fashion "Soft & Shimmering Silver & White!" #2252. $300.00.

1981 Superstar Barbie Festival #3240 (Spain) has platinum blonde hair, and she wears a shimmering blue evening ensemble with one sleeve trimmed in silver, a blue net overskirt, and blue ankle-strap shoes. $400.00.

1981 Superstar Barbie Hollywood #9720 (Spain) wears the original hot pink SuperStar Barbie gown and boa in a different fabric. $300.00.

1981 Superstar Barbie Novia #9907 (Spain) wears a lacy ivory wedding gown with veil very similar to the ensemble worn by the 1976 European Beautiful Bride Barbie. $300.00.

1981 Western Barbie #3469 (Spain) uses the SuperStar Barbie head mold, but this European version does not have the winking eye feature found on American dolls, nor does this Spanish version have the busy hands found on the Western Barbie with the non-winking SuperStar face sold throughout Europe. $75.00.

The American Western Barbie with the winking eye is shown for comparison.

1982 Barbie #5336 uses the SuperStar Barbie head mold with golden blonde straight hair parted on her left and a pale skin tone. She has unbending legs and wears a one-piece swimsuit featuring a blue and white striped top, a lavender waistband, and blue bottoms. $45.00.

1982 Barbie #5336 was also sold in a hot pink one-piece swimsuit. $50.00.

1982 Gran Gala Barbie #3868 (Spain) has platinum hair, a rosier skin tone, and different facial paint screening than the American Dream Date Barbie. $50.00.

1982 Movie Date Barbie #4530 wears a purple halter sundress with pink trim, mirrored purple sunglasses, and purple open-toe heels. This outfit was sold as a carded Fashion Fun Barbie fashion in the U.S. $40.00.

1982 Super Dance Barbie #5838 (Spain) has platinum hair and tan skin. She wears a purple leotard with leggings, a headband, and shoes. The Super Dance/Super Sport dolls were also sold in other European countries but without the free child's headband and with less dramatic facial paint and hair colors. $35.00.

1982 Super Dance Skipper #5840 (Spain) wears a purple dance costume, and she comes with purple leggings, a purple headband, and sneakers. This Spanish version has pale blonde waist-length hair and tan skin, and a free headband is included for the child. $80.00.

The Spanish Skipper and European Skipper close-ups are shown for comparison.

1982 Super Sport Ken #5839 (Spain) wears white gym shorts trimmed in purple, a purple t-shirt featuring lavender short sleeves, white socks, and white sneakers. A purple headband is included for Ken, and this version from Spain includes a free headband for the child. $55.00.

1981 Safari Skipper #4975 wears a brown minidress with a shiny gold belt. A brown hat and flats complete her costurme. $95.00.

1983 Ballerina Barbie #4983. The classic Ballerina Barbie sold in the U.S. from 1976 to 1979 with the Twist 'N Turn Barbie head mold was revived in Europe in 1983 with the SuperStar Barbie face mold and a revised white ballerina costume with sparkly tulle skirt. This newer doll uses the classic ballerina arms and a shiny silver crown and is able to dance like a prima ballerina with her poseable body and two-piece stand. $55.00.

1983 Bridal Barbie #4799 wears a white satin blouse covered by white lace, a white satin skirt, and a tulle veil with a floral headband. She carries a bouquet of pink plastic flowers. This is the same wedding ensemble worn by Barbie doll's friend Tracy in the U.S. $75.00.

1983 Crystal Barbie #4598 (Spain) has platinum hair, a rosier skin tone, pale pink lips, and different facial paint screening than the American Crystal Barbie. $45.00.

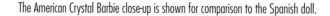

The American Crystal Barbie close-up is shown for comparison to the Spanish doll.

1983 Mille Luci Christie #4859 (Italy) is identical to the American African-American Crystal Barbie, but in Italy she is Barbie doll's black friend Christie. She wears an iridescent white ballgown with a shimmering white boa and rhinestone jewelry. $85.00.

1983 Fabulous Fur Barbie #7093 has brown streaks in her blonde hair. She wears a spectacular glittery blue bodysuit with iridescent white belt and transformable full-length white faux fur coat. $65.00.

1983 Fantaisie Barbie #7193 (France) has platinum center-parted hair with the SuperStar Barbie head mold and pink skin. Her box has the "TV" symbol to denote television advertising. $45.00 each.

1983 Fashion Play Barbie #7193 is a collection of six basic Barbie dolls, with the SuperStar Barbie face, tan skin, and blonde hair parted on their left, wearing inexpensive fashions. Their box backs state, "6 dolls, each in her own pretty fashion!" $35.00 each.

1983 Fashion Play Barbie #7193, released in 1984, is a collection of four basic Barbie dolls with the SuperStar Barbie head mold, blue eyes, and blonde hair that is curly on the ends. Their box backs state, "4 dolls, each in her own pretty fashion!" $35.00 each.

1983 Fashion Play Barbie #7193, released in 1984, is another collection of dolls using the SuperStar Barbie head mold wearing an assortment of fashions. $35.00 each.

1983 Fruhlingszauber Barbie #7546 (Germany) wears a long white gown decorated with pink and purple stripes, pink and purple flowers, and a ruffled boa. A white hat with pink hatband, pink pumps, and a white flower basket with flowers completes her ensemble. This fashion was sold as a boxed "Springtime Magic" fashion in the U.S. $75.00.

1983 Great Shape Barbie #7311 (England) wears a green full body leotard with yellow sash, a green headband, and yellow ballet slippers. She comes with an exercise bag and exercise booklet. The American Great Shape Barbie wears a blue leotard with pink sash. $40.00.

1983 Great Shape Ken #7310 (England) wears green workout pants, a white t-shirt featuring green and yellow stripes, and white sneakers. The American version wears blue workout pants. $40.00.

1983 Great Shape Skipper #7312 (England) wears a green leotard with a yellow sash and green and yellow striped leg warmers, while the American edition wears a pink and blue version of this costume. $45.00.

1983 Mode Fantaisie Barbie #264 (France) uses the same SuperStar Barbie head with pink skin as used on the 1977 – 1979 SuperStar Barbie doll. The box side has the "Club Des Amies De Barbie" logo with an illustration of Barbie doll's face, and a club enrollment form is included. The box back shows six dolls in this series. $65.00.

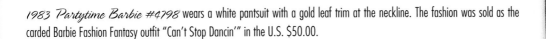

1983 Partytime Barbie #4798 wears a white pantsuit with a gold leaf trim at the neckline. The fashion was sold as the carded Barbie Fashion Fantasy outfit "Can't Stop Dancin'" in the U.S. $50.00.

1983 Pretty Party Barbie #7194 wears a white bodice with lace border and attached lavender skirt with sheer overskirt and purple satin waistband. $50.00.

1984 5th Aniversario Barbie #23061 (Spain) wears a purple and white party dress with a "Barbie 5 Aniversario" sash. She is packaged with an extra dress and a pink "Barbie" pencil. $175.00.

1984 Beach Time Barbie #9102 wears a red swimsuit with a ruffle at the bodice and a white tie-on skirt. $25.00.

1984 Beach Time Ken # 9103 wears red swim trunks and a red mesh shirt. $25.00.

1984 Beach Time Skipper #9104 wears a red swimsuit with a red and white skirt. $40.00.

1984 Sea Lovin' Barbie #9109 wears a red, white, and blue striped shirt with an anchor-design collar, a white miniskirt with blue stars, and white sneakers. She comes with a white duffle bag. $45.00.

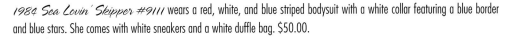

1984 Sea Lovin' Ken #9110 wears a red, white, and blue striped shirt exposing a bare midriff, white sailor shorts, and white sneakers. He comes with a cloth duffle bag. $40.00.

1984 Sea Lovin' Skipper #9111 wears a red, white, and blue striped bodysuit with a white collar featuring a blue border and blue stars. She comes with white sneakers and a white duffle bag. $50.00.

1985 Le Nouveau Theatre De La Mode Barbie (France) was created by Billy Boy for Mattel France to commemorate the first Barbie Retrospective exhibit in Paris, France, in May 1985. Barbie doll wears a black crepe sheath dress with a gold chain necklace, gold hoop earrings, and a gold bracelet. Black sunglasses and shoes comlete her ensemble. These dolls are individually numbered in an edition of 10,000. Five hundred of the dolls were given black fingernail polish and were personally autographed by Billy Boy. $175.00.

1985 *Music Lovin' Barbie* #9988 wears a yellow bodysuit with a knit yellow and white jacket and yellow and white leg warmers. Each doll in this series comes with a play Walkman stereo with headset and two cassettes that actually fit in the player. $35.00.

1985 *Music Lovin' Ken* #2388 wears a white leather-look "Ken" logo jacket with yellow sleeves, yellow sweatpants, and white sneakers. $35.00.

1985 *Music Lovin' Skipper* #2854 wears a yellow bodysuit with a knit yellow and white jacket and yellow and white leg warmers. $50.00.

1985 *My First Barbie Sa Premiere* includes a pink vinyl "B" logo carry case that contains My First Barbie #1875 in a white dress with pink accents, My First Barbie Easy-on Fashions #2121 (a pink nightshirt with leggings and slippers), and the Barbie Dream Furniture Collection Vanity & Seat #2469. $100.00.

1985 Tropical Marina #2056 is Barbie doll's exotic island friend. She uses the Oriental Barbie head mold with center-parted knee-length black hair, and she wears a one-piece dark floral swimsuit with a yellow hair ruffle. The doll is called Tropical Miko in the U.S., and all later American Miko dolls have European counterparts called Marina. $30.00.

1985 Rock Stars Derek #2478 (Spain) is similar to the U.S. Rocker Derek, but this Spanish version has unbending straight arms and a non-twisting waist, and his skin tone and facial paint screening are different. $75.00.

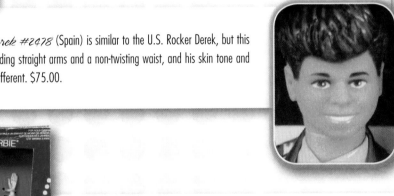

1986 Rock Stars Barbie #3055 (Italy) wears a pink miniskirt with shiny silver stars, a matching top featuring the "ROCKERS" logo, silver lamé pants, silver star earrings, sparkly clear pumps, and a pink wrist band with fringe. She comes with a Barbie Rock Stars Compilation cassette tape that was not included with the same doll sold in other countries. The tape includes eight songs. $35.00.

1986 Rock Stars Ken #3131 (Spain) debuts the new Ken head mold with rooted blond hair and blue eyes. He wears a silver lamé duster coat over a jump-suit featuring silver pants and a white "ROCK STARS" shirt, a silver lamé scarf, and a single pink glove. This Spanish version uses straight arms and a non-twisting waist, and his complexion and facial paint screening differ from the American Rocker Ken. $85.00.

1986 Fashion Play/Pool Side Barbie #3076 wears a yellow bodysuit with a blue and red sash. $20.00.

1986 Fashion Play/Uptown Barbie #3074 wears a pink dress with a pink ruffle on the bodice. $20.00.

1986 Fashion Play/Hostess Barbie #3077 (Canada) wears a lavender dress with white trim on the bodice and white hearts on the waistband. In Canada the Fashion Play dolls have individual names like Hostess to identify each doll. $20.00.

1986 Fashion Play/Party Cruise Barbie #3075 (Canada) wears a multicolor striped one-piece swimsuit with a white coverup. $20.00.

1986 Diamantes Skipper #3133 (Spain) uses the original pre-pubescent 1964 Skipper body, while her counterpart in the U.S., Jewel Secrets Skipper, uses the 1978 Super Teen body. Her facial paint is different in Spain, and the Spanish doll has cascading, wavy hair while the American version has tight ringlet curls in the classic Shirley Temple style. $65.00.

The American Jewel Secrets Skipper close-up is shown for comparison.

1986 Princess Laura #3179 is identical to the American Jewel Secrets Whitney, but in Europe Whitney was called Laura. She uses the Steffie head mold with thigh-length braided brown hair. She wears a sparkly slim blue dress with a silver jacket, a shiny silver belt, and a silver tiara with blue jewels. $65.00.

1986 Princess Laura Fashions #1862 is the only separately packaged fashion sold for Laura. It includes a silver lamé minidress, a blue lamé skirt, silver fingerless gloves, blue pumps, and a silver mask. $35.00.

1986 Tennis Barbie #1760 wears a pink and white tennis fashion with gold trim. She comes with a tennis racket, socks, and pink sneakers. $30.00.

1986 Tennis Ken #1761 wears blue shorts, a white shirt with gold stripes and a blue collar, white socks, and blue sneakers. He comes with a tennis racket. $30.00.

1986 Tennis Skipper #1762 wears a purple and white tennis fashion with gold trim. White socks, purple sneakers, and a tennis racket are included. $35.00.

1987 Barbie and the Bi Bops Becky #4967 uses the Diva head mold with sandy blonde hair worn in a 1950s handlebars hairstyle. She is identical to the American Barbie and the Sensations Bopsy, but in Europe Bopsy is called Becky. $50.00.

1987 Barbie and the Bi Bops Bibi #4977 uses the Oriental Barbie head mold. She is identical to the American Barbie and the Sensations Becky, but in Europe Becky is called Bibi. $50.00.

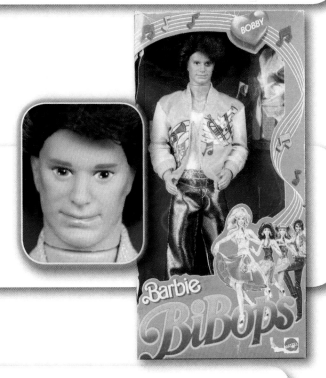

1987 Barbie and the Bi Bops Bobby #4960 uses the Rocker Ken head mold with rooted auburn hair and blue eyes. Bobby wears purple metallic pants with a silver shirt and a yellow and white letterman jacket. A microphone, sunglasses, and shoes are included. Bobby was only available in Europe; in America African-American Belinda was the fourth member of the Sensations quartet. $75.00.

1987 Barbie and the Bi Bops Fashions #4990 is the only separate fashion created for Bi Bops Bobby. Blue satin pants are attached to a sleeveless yellow satin shirt with a pink bowtie and a pink cummerbund, and a flashy metallic-print jacket with shimmering blue lapels and navy blue shoes complete the ensemble. $100.00.

1987 California Skipper #4440 wears a blue one-piece swimsuit under white overalls featuring white and yellow striped legs and a record, musical note, and polka dot print. A yellow California flag, yellow sneakers, a blue Frisbee, a blue headband, and a comic book are included. $55.00.

#4834

1987 Fashion Play Barbie dolls are called "fun & frilly" on the box backs. Four styles were available. $25.00 each.

#4830

#4854

#4835

1987 Meine Erste Barbie-Set #8790 (Germany) packages the My First Barbie ballerina with the blue dress sold separately as My First Barbie Fashions #1895 and a unique ballet dance cassette tape in a pink suitcase-style package. $40.00.

1987 My First Barbie Set #5386 (France) packages the My First Barbie ballerina with My First Barbie Fashions #1876, a white floral-print skirt with attached pink top, and a "MA PREMIERE BARBIE DANSE A L'OPERA" cassette tape. $40.00.

1987 Party Pink Barbie #4629 wears a long slim pink skirt and bodice with a matching pink train/cape, a pink faux fur stole, a silver belt, pink tights, and pink pumps. Her costume transforms for many different looks. This doll was sold in the U.S. as Wal-Mart's Pink Jubilee Barbie. $18.00.

1987 Top Model Barbie #6750 (Spain) has tan skin and platinum hair parted on her left and worn in two banded sections. She wears an iridescent aqua dress with a blue flounce with pink hem. $55.00.

1988 1 + 2 Barbie #8590 packages the Dress Me Barbie wearing pink lingerie with white lace trim with two additional carded Barbie fashions. $38.00.

1988 Chic Barbie #6251 (Spain) wears a white bubble dress with green polka-dots and a green satin waistband and white pumps. $40.00.

1988 Fashion Play Barbie #1380 wears a knee-length pale blue dress with iridescent and net overskirts and blue pumps. $22.00.

1988 Fashion Play Barbie #1376 wears a pink dress with pink and silver overskirt panels and pink pumps. $22.00.

1988 St. Tropez Barbie #2096 wears a pink and black one-piece swimsuit decorated with shiny silver stars. $20.00.

1988 Super Style Barbie #2937 introduces WondraCurl hair — hair that is supposed to hold styles without hairspray or wetting. She wears a dress with a denim bodice adorned with a pink jewel and a layered confetti-design pink skirt and wrap, along with a matching ruffle in her two-tone hair. A styling wand, denim handbag, and pumps are included. $35.00.

1988 Super Style Skipper #1915 has two-tone WondraCurl hair and wears a dress with a denim bodice and a peach confetti-design skirt, wrap, and hair ruffle. A styling wand, denim handbag, and shoes are included. $35.00.

1989 1 + 2 Barbie #8590 packages Dress Me Barbie wearing pale pink lingerie with two additional carded fashions. $35.00.

1989 5th Aniversario Barbie Em Portugal #6139 (Portugal) was designed by Augustus. She wears a silver-speckled white dress over layers of tulle and a matching jacket. $135.00.

1989 10th Aniversario Barbie #6747 (Spain) was designed by Manuel Pertegaz. Barbie wears a dramatic red gown with roses on the bodice and train. $125.00.

1989 Fashion Play Barbie #7231 wears a pink minidress featuring a single sleeve with silver designs, a matching short overskirt, and pink pumps. $22.00.

1989 Fashion Play Barbie #7232 wears a lavender skirt with an iridescent bodice and lavender pumps. $25.00.

1989 Ma Première Barbie Miniclub (France) is the fan club doll for France's Barbie Miniclub. Barbie wears a white ballerina outfit with a hairbow and ballet slippers; this is the same doll sold in the U.S. in 1989 as My First Barbie, but this French edition includes an automatic nine-month subscription to the Barbie Miniclub. A letter from Barbie and three cards showing Barbie dancing are included. $30.00.

1989 My First Barbie Princess #9942 wears an iridescent white floral-design skirt with matching ruffle sleeves, a pink bodice, an iridescent white tiara, and pink pumps. The American version of this doll has a purple bodice. $35.00.

1989 Sports Club Ken 9362 wears a blue shirt with a white collar panel featuring stars, blue knee-length golf pants, knee-high white socks, and sneakers. He carries a cloth golf bag that transforms into blue pants. He comes with a golf club, golf balls, a putting dish, and a can of soda. While this European Ken is a golfer, the American All Stars Ken is a basketball player. $50.00.

1989 All Stars Ken #9361 from the U.S. is shown for comparison. $20.00.

● ● ● ● ● ●

1989 Riviera Barbie #7344 wears a pink and green one-piece swimsuit with black trim. $25.00.

1989 Happy Holidays Barbie Store Display (Germany) features Happy Holidays Barbie in her red gown against a mirror-finish backing in a cardboard display framed with lights. The upper left corner has the "JUBILAUMS BARBIE 1959 – 1989 30 JAHRE BARBIE" logo, which recognizes the 30th anniversary of Barbie. Although the Happy Holidays Barbie in the red dress debuted in the U.S. in 1988, Europe released their Happy Holidays Barbie dolls a year later. $295.00.

1990 Happy Holidays Barbie Store Display (Germany) features Happy Holidays Barbie in her white gown with white faux fur trim and dramatic red jewelry set against a shiny red backdrop inside a white cardboard display framed with twinkling lights. This Happy Holidays Barbie in the white gown debuted in the U.S. in 1989, but the European edition, virtually an identical doll except for the packaging, debuted one year later. $250.00.

1990 Auguri Da Barbie #0672 (Italy) is a special Italian Christmas gift set which repackages the 1990 Happy Holidays Barbie with a 1990 Barbie Couturier (Private Collection) Fashion. $65.00.

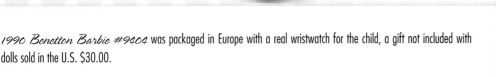

1990 Benetton Barbie #9404 was packaged in Europe with a real wristwatch for the child, a gift not included with dolls sold in the U.S. $30.00.

1990 Benetton Ken #9406 wears orange pants; a blue shirt covered by an orange, blue, and green tank top; an orange bandana; orange socks; and a striped purple jacket. An orange hat and purple shoes complete his ensemble. Created for Europe, Benetton Ken had very limited distribution in the U.S. as a Barbie Pink Stamp Club premium. $30.00.

1990 Benetton Teresa #9408 uses the Steffie head mold with brown eyes and red lips. She wears an orange top, blue shorts, orange stockings, a yellow and black scarf, yellow hoop earrings, a quilted-look multicolor jacket, blue and red leggings, and yellow sneakers. $65.00.

1990 Capri Barbie #5733 wears a one-piece swimsuit featuring a pink print tank top with attached black shorts with white polka dots. $25.00.

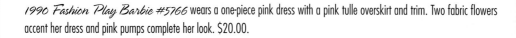

1990 Fashion Play Barbie #5734 wears a purple and white fashion with a purple skirt and a white bodice with a ruffle featuring purple floral designs and pink dots. $20.00.

1990 Fashion Play Barbie #5766 wears a one-piece pink dress with a pink tulle overskirt and trim. Two fabric flowers accent her dress and pink pumps complete her look. $20.00.

1990 Happy Birthday Barbie wears a pink party gown featuring layered pink skirts, an iridescent white shawl, a pink jewel choker that doubles as a ring for the child, and pink pumps. She has iridescent strands rooted in her hair, and she comes with a gift box containing a pendant gift for the child. $50.00.

1990 On-the-Go Barbie #1307 wears a white top with a purple and pink star-print skirt and a matching jacket. She has pink star-shaped earrings and pink sneakers. A carry-all and fashion stick-ons are included. $45.00.

1990 Friendship Barbie #5506 (Germany) commemorates the fall of the Berlin Wall and the reunification of Germany. Dressed in a short pink dress with iridescent white ruffle, she was the first Barbie doll seen by many East German children. $25.00.

1990 Friendship Barbie #2080 (Germany) wears a black "B" logo t-shirt with an attached pink skirt and a white jacket. This is the same fashion worn by the U.S. 1989 Dance Club Barbie. $25.00.

1991 Friendship Barbie #3677 is the third doll in the Friendship collection commemorating the reunification of East Germany and West Germany. She was distributed throughout Europe while the first two editions were offered primarily in Germany. Barbie doll wears a pretty red velvet bodice with sheer white sleeves adorned with red hearts, a white skirt with sheer overskirt covered with red hearts, and red pumps. Her costume is an abbreviated version of the classic 1983 Loving You Barbie doll's gown. $30.00.

1991 Barbie Li'l Friends are a series of five toddler girls who use the Heart Family baby's head and body molds. The box back calls them "adorable little friends for Barbie and you!" $35.00 each.

#2202

#2203

#2204

#2205

#2206

1991 Barbie Li'l Friend & Rocking Horse #2150 includes a brown-haired blue-eyed girl wearing a purple shirt with an attached white skirt. A rocking horse is included. $75.00.

1991 Barbie Li'l Friend & Wagon #2152 includes a blonde brown-eyed girl wearing a blue top with an attached print skirt. A wagon is included. $75.00.

1991 Barbie Li'l Friend & Walker #2153 includes a blonde, blue-eyed child wearing a pink top with multicolored pants. A walker is included. $75.00.

1991 Benetton Shopping Barbie #4873 wears a yellow top, a white miniskirt with red belt, a red jacket with purple trim, red hoop earrings, black and white leggings, a yellow and red scarf, a black and white checked beret with red trim, a purple fanny pack, and red boots. $30.00.

1991 Benetton Shopping Ken #4876 has two-tone blonde hair and wears red corduroy pants, a blue shirt, a brown suede-look jacket with orange collar and cuffs, and blue sneakers. $70.00.

1991 Benetton Shopping Christie #4887 wears an orange and red knit sweater, a blue miniskirt, orange leggings, a blue wrap, orange hoop earrings, a blue and red hat, and red sneakers. $85.00.

1991 Benetton Shopping Marina #4898 uses the Oriental Barbie head mold. Marina wears a pink top, a plaid miniskirt, a purple coat with plaid lapels, purple hoop earrings, a pink knit hat, pink leggings, plaid socks, and purple sneakers. $150.00.

1991 Benetton Shopping Teresa #4880 wears a blue bodysuit, green shortalls, blue hoop earrings, yellow socks, a quilted yellow coat, a yellow and green cap, and blue sneakers. She uses the Steffie head mold. $150.00.

1991 Benetton Shopping Fashions were sold exclusively in Europe in 1991. Three unique new fashions were available, each modeled by a different Benetton Shopping doll on the box photos. $50.00 each.

#5962

#5963

#5964

1991 Dream Bride Barbie #5466 is arguably the most beautiful bridal Barbie ever. Her box back states, "Sparkling with beauty, the bride appears. It's Barbie, exquisite in a sparkling gown of sequins and roses. But for now it is only a beautiful dream!" Since Barbie doll's debut in 1959, Mattel has never officially allowed Barbie doll to marry, but she often dreams of the happy occasion! $100.00.

1991 Ibiza Barbie #4218 wears a one-piece white swimsuit with pink midriff and attached miniskirt and pink pumps. $20.00.

1991 Maoni #1750 debuts a new ethnic head mold. Maoni is known as Shani in the U.S., and Mattel boasts that the doll has an ethnically correct skin tone, facial features, and hair color and texture. Maoni is a top model, and her one-piece pink, blue, and red swimsuit features gold glitter and a gold collar. She also wears a matching dress with net overskirt that transforms into a cover-up, gold dangle earrings, a hair jewel/necklace/belt accessory, and purple pumps. $38.00.

1991 Teen Talk Ich Spreche Mit Dir Barbie #4767 (Germany) has a honey-blonde no-bangs crimped hairstyle not used for Teen Talk Barbie dolls sold in the U.S. $55.00.

1991 Teen Talk Je Te Parle Barbie #4709 (France) has blonde hair in the hairstyle used on the American redhead Teen Talk Barbie; no red-headed Teen Talk Barbie dolls were sold in Europe. $55.00.

1991 Ultra Hair Whitney #7736 uses the Steffie head mold with blue eyes, pink lips, and ankle-length brown hair. She wears a blue Pucci-style dress with blue earrings. In the U.S. the doll was sold as brunette Totally Hair Barbie, but that American doll has the SuperStar Barbie head mold. $75.00.

The close-up of the American Totally Hair Barbie is shown for comparison.

1992 Barbie Li'l Friends is a series of four girls using the Heart Family babies' head and body molds. $25.00 each.

#3536

#3537

#3539

#3538

1992 Earring Magic Midge #7018 has crimped red hair with bangs accented with a gold hair band. Midge wears a blue leather-look dress with sheer sleeves, a gold belt with charms, and gold earrings. In the U.S. Earring Magic Midge wears a yellow version of this blue dress. $38.00.

1992 Party Changes Barbie #2505 wears a rose satin bodice and pink layered petal skirt that can be worn four different ways. $25.00.

1992 Style Barbie #2454 wears a purple and orange striped top with attached orange skirt with purple polka dots. A red satin hairbow, a purple bow on the skirt, and purple pumps complement the ensemble. $28.00.

1992 Tahiti Barbie #2093 wears a colorful multicolor print pink dress with pink pumps. $25.00.

1992 Disney Weekend Barbie #10722 wears a white Mickey Mouse dress with an attached black miniskirt with white polka dots, matching sleeves, and a Mickey Mouse ears hat. She was created for the Euro Disney theme park. $40.00

1993 Disney Weekend Barbie #10723 wears a green and pink Minnie and Mickey t-shirt with a pink skirt and a Mickey Mouse ears hat. A pink Daisy Duck shirt and yellow shorts are included for a second look. $35.00.

1993 Disney Weekend Barbie & Ken #10724 includes Ken doll wearing a white Mickey t-shirt with white paint-splotch pants with blue pockets and Barbie doll wearing a red Minnie t-shirt with a white paint-splotch skirt with blue ruffle. Both dolls have Mickey Mouse ears hats. $65.00.

1993 Bali Barbie #10776 wears a multicolored print playsuit with pink waistband and pink pumps. $18.00.

1993 Barbie Li'l Friends is a third edition series of Li'l Friends who are often identi-fied as Barbie doll's "nieces" since the line "Les Nieces de Barbie" appears on the box front. Three toddler girls and one toddler boy comprise this series. $20.00 each.

#11853

#11854

#11855

#11856

1993 Gymnast Barbie #11921 uses the bend-and-move body and has a pink satin ribbon in her braided hair. She wears a pink workout costume with white socks and pink gym shoes. She is packaged with a blue towel, a pink duffle bag, a gold medal, a pink headband, pink armbands, and weights. The blue towel, headband, and armbands were not included with the American edition. $20.00.

1993 Jewel & Glitter Barbie #11185 wears a gold lamé top and a black vest with black skirt that reverse to pink. Sequins, stencils, and fabric paint are included to decorate Barbie doll and her costume. The Jewel & Glitter dolls were not sold in the U.S. but their costumes were available as boxed fashions. $30.00.

1993 Jewel & Glitter Teresa #11214 has red hair and green eyes. She wears a purple skirt and top that reverse to green. $28.00.

1993 Jewel & Glitter Shani #11215 wears an orange skirt and jacket that reverse to yellow. A gold lamé top and orange pumps complete her ensemble. $45.00.

1993 Locket Surprise Alexia #11209 is known as Kayla in the U.S. Rare Alexia uses the Teresa head mold with waist-length red hair. She has a hollow blue chest compartment that holds heart-shaped containers of cosmetics or a photo of Barbie. A blue ruffle at the bodice, a sparkly blue floral-print layered skirt, silver earrings, and blue pumps complete her ensemble. $100.00.

1993 Magical Hair Mermaid Barbie #11570 has rooted purple hair that turns pink in the water. She wears an iridescent mermaid costume with fish tail, matching bodice adorned with pearls, and a headdress with pearls. $50.00.

1993 Naf Naf Barbie #10997 wears designer Naf Naf clothing, including a pink Naf Naf coat, an orange tank top, yellow leggings, a denim skirt, blue Naf Naf earrings, and a yellow and red NAF NAF Barbie cap. A purple NAF NAF minidress, stickers, purple sneakers, pink sneakers, and a nylon bag are included. $35.00.

1993 Naf Naf Ken #10998 wears NAF NAF jeans and a matching jean jacket, a yellow shirt, and a NAF NAF cap. He comes with green NAF NAF swim trunks, a NAF NAF backpack, and sneakers. $45.00.

1993 Naf Naf Midge #10999 wears a colorful NAF NAF flag-print suit with lacy white shirt, a yellow tank top, yellow NAF NAF earrings, and a red NAF NAF cap. She comes with an orange NAF NAF minidress, a round travel bag, and two pairs of shoes. $55.00.

1993 Spielzeug-Ring Secret Hearts Barbie Deluxe Gift Set #10929 (Germany) commemorates the 25th anniversary of the Spielzeug-Ring store of Germany. A "25 Jahre SPIELZEUG RING" sticker is on the box window, and a "Mattel GmbH of West Germany" sticker is on the box bottom. Except for the stickers, the dolls are identical to the set sold in the U.S. $65.00.

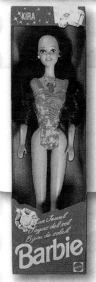

1993 Sun Jewel Kira #19056 is unlike any other Kira doll because she has the SuperStar Barbie head mold. Every other Kira doll has the Oriental Barbie head mold. She wears the glittery orange and pink floral-print one-piece swimsuit and necklace of Glitter Beach Kira, sold one year earlier. Several of these identical dolls were discovered in this three-language Sun Jewel Kira box, so apparently an entire production run of this doll with the SuperStar head was created for one European country. $125.00.

1993 Vedes Star Barbie #11643 (Germany) commemorates the 90th anniversary of the Vedes store. She wears a pink and silver gown, fingerless silver lamé gloves, and a white satin "Vedes Star Barbie" banner and a "Vedes 90 Jahre" hangtag. $45.00.

1994 Barbie Style #12291 wears a white and turquoise tennis fashion with visor. A tennis racket, sneakers, and a gold necklace for the child are included. $25.00.

1994 Baywatch Teresa #13201. Based on the popular television show, Baywatch Teresa wears a blue Baywatch hooded jacket and pants and comes with a red Baywatch swimsuit, yellow sneakers, a visor, binoculars, a rescue buoy, whistle, a Frisbee, and a rescue board that makes realistic motor sounds. $35.00.

1994 Butterfly Prince Ken #13237 uses a modified 1990-dated Ken head mold with rooted brown hair. He wears a shimmery black tuxedo with pink bowtie and pink cummerbund. He has flowers and a magical butterfly for Barbie. $30.00.

1994 Dance Moves Midge #13085 uses the Diva head mold with dark red crimped hair. She has the bend-and-move body and wears a glittery blue top, metallic blue shorts with iridescent suspenders, glittery blue tights, and black shoes. A radio, a microphone, and a cassette player with headphones are included. In Europe, Dance Moves Midge replaced the American African-American Dance Moves Barbie, but both dolls wear identical costumes. $36.00.

1994 Disney Fun Barbie #12957 wears blue Mickey Mouse and floral-print pants with a denim-look jacket featuring matching panels, a pink and white gingham shirt, a matching hairbow, and pink hoop earrings. She carries a pink Mickey Mouse purse. $28.00.

1994 Horse Riding Barbie #12456 is dressed for riding her walking horse, Sprint, wearing silver riding pants with a blue and purple satin jacket with silver lamé collar and cuffs, a pink scarf, and black riding boots. She has the bend-and-move body and holds a riding crop and comes with a hat and a silver trophy. $40.00.

1994 Happy Holidays Barbie #12432 wears a red gown with a white faux fur collar and cuffs and a faux fur white hat adorned with a red poinsettia. This is the first Happy Holidays Barbie created exclusively for Europe. $72.00.

1994 Shelly #12489 is the "Cute baby sister of Barbie!" This first edition Shelly debuted in 1995 wearing a pink sleeper with a pink flower on the bodice. She is packaged with a white crib with mobile, blanket, an extra black dress with white lace trim, white tights, black shoes, a rattle, a jar of baby food, a bottle, a food tray, a pink plastic bunny, and a brush. In the U.S., Shelly is known as Kelly. $30.00.

1995 Barbie At Harvey Nichols #0175 is an edition of only 250 dolls created for the Harvey Nichols store in London. The doll is a blonde 35th Anniversary Barbie re-dressed in a black dress, pink silk shantung jacket, pink marabou-trimmed scarf, and black patent leather belt. A black purse, sunglasses, and shoes are included. The story on her box states that Barbie spent her 36th birthday in London. $400.00.

1995 Barbie Pez Autogrill Toys #17190 (Italy) is exclusive to the Autogrill Toys stores in Italy. Barbie doll wears a black knit top with a red plaid skirt, red pantyhose, an apple necklace, a red headband, and black boots. $35.00.

1995 Braut Barbie #13614 (Germany) wears a white dotted Swiss bridal gown trimmed in pink gingham piping and a veil with a pink gingham headband. She carries a daisy bouquet. Braut Barbie was originally intended to be a Vedes store exclusive in Europe but was sold by most toy retailers in Germany. $20.00.

1995 Barbie Style #10804 wears a black and white vertically striped empire-waist skirt featuring pink floral print with an attached pink top accented by a black bow. $20.00.

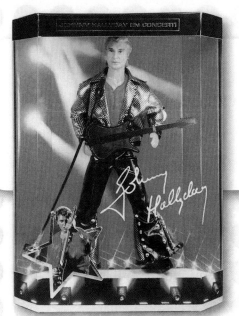

1995 Johnny Hallyday En Concert #14069 (France) immortalizes French singer Johnny Hallyday on the 35th anniversary of his career using a newly sculpted head mold in Hallyday's likeness with a Ken doll body. He wears black leather pants, a red shirt, a silver lamé jacket, and boots, and he has a golden earring in his left earlobe. A floor microphone, a guitar, and a numbered certificate of authenticity are included. According to his box, Johnny Hallyday sold over 80 million records, released 50 albums, and performed at more than 400 concerts for 15 million fans since his 1960 stage debut. $125.00.

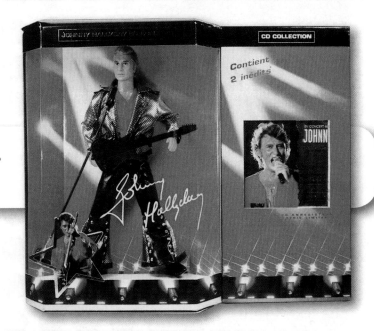

1995 Johnny Hallyday En Concert CD Collection #62210 packages the doll with an "En Concert" CD collection of his songs. $150.00.

1995 Jose Carreras Doctora Barbie #11160 promotes the Jose Carreras Foundation for fighting leukemia. Jose Carreras is pictured on the box holding Doctora Barbie, and a blue pretend doctor's ID badge with a "Jose Carreras Barbie y tu" heart logo is included. $70.00.

1995 Li'l Friends of Shelly Susie #14854 is known as Melody in the U.S. $35.00. Courtesy of Laurel Willoughby.

1995 Super Gymnast Barbie #15821 wears a white, pink, and blue gymnast costume featuring star accents, a "gold" medal on a pink ribbon, white socks, and white sneakers. A tumbling ring is included to allow Barbie to perform gymnastics with her bend-and-move body. $18.00.

1995 Happy Holidays Barbie #13545 wears a dark green velvety top with a white satin skirt featuring green and red stripes with gold threading. She wears a matching hair bow and carries a white faux fur muffler. $40.00.

1996 Happy Holidays Barbie #15816 wears a red and green plaid taffeta skirt with a green satin top featuring a white faux fur collar and cuffs and a lace-up bodice. A hairbow matching her skirt is in her hair. $35.00.

1996 Andalucia Barbie (Spain) #15758 was designed by Pepe Jimenez, a famous fashion designer from Spain's Andalucia region. The colors of Barbie doll's flaménco dress and multiple tiers of ruffles are authentic to the Andalucia region. She uses the SuperStar Barbie head mold. $30.00.

1996 Blokker Barbie #15611 commemorates the 100th anniversary of the Blokker organization in the Netherlands. She wears a pink satin dress with sheer tiered overskirts, a lacy bodice featuring a single pink rose and ruffled sleeves, and a pearl necklace. $45.00.

1996 Easy Chic Barbie #17590 (England) was designed by Luigi Avenoso, winner of the 1996 Barbie Fashion Awards Business/Professional category; his winning design is modeled by this doll. Easy Chic Barbie wears a black two-piece suit with white lining and a black and white marabou hat. Sunglasses, short white gloves, black pumps, and a black handbag complete the ensemble. $395.00.

1996 Gardaland Barbie #14650 (Italy) is exclusive to Italy's Gardaland amusement park. She wears a black top with a striped pink satin jacket, a matching skirt with black waistband, and pink sneakers. A 4,000 lire coupon for park admission is included. $36.00.

1996 Happy Holidays Barbie Noel #15646 (France) packages the 1996 Happy Holidays Barbie with Sacha Distel's "Noel" CD. The CD features 12 holiday tunes sung in French, including "White Christmas," "Silent Night," and "Jingle Bells." $100.00.

1996 Palmers Barbie (Austria) is exclusive to the Palmers clothing store in Austria. Palmers Barbie wears a green employee's uniform with a white P-logo blouse. She comes with panties, a bra, a Palmers shopping bag, shoes, and a green ten-shilling Palmers token. Only 1,500 dolls were made. $95.00.

1996 Palmers Barbie Second Edition (Austria) wears an employee apprentice uniform, a white shirt with a green pleated skirt, a green hair bow, and a garter. She comes with a scarf decorated with the Palmers horse-drawn coach, a Palmers shopping bag, and a green ten-shilling Palmers token. Only 1,300 dolls were made. $85.00.

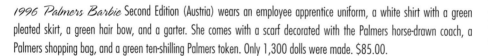

1997 Palmers Barbie Third Edition (Austria) is a re-dressed Splash 'n Color Teresa wearing a white bikini with a sheer black cover-up. A P-logo white towel, a Palmers shopping bag, black sunglasses, a green ten-shilling Palmers token, and a poster featuring a model wearing a life-size version of this fashion are included. Only 2,500 dolls were made. $72.00.

1997 Palmers Barbie Fourth Edition (Austria) wears a sheer white nightgown with panties, a white satin robe, and golden angel wings. She comes with a white pillow, a Palmers shopping bag, a poster of a model wearing this fashion, a green Palmers 10-shilling token, and a golden Palmers token dated 1997. $70.00.

1998 Palmers Barbie Fifth Edition (Austria) wears a green carriage driver's uniform with a green top hat, white stockings, and black boots. She comes with a Palmers Christmas card, a Palmers shopping bag, a green Palmers 10-shilling token, and a golden five-Euro token. $65.00.

1999 Palmers Millennium Barbie (Austria) uses the Mackie head mold. She wears a holographic silver skirt with a "jeweled" bra, a gray jacket with "jeweled" trim, holographic silver boots, and a matching hair band. A silver "2000" memory book and a green Palmers five-Deutsche mark token are included. $75.00.

1996 West End Barbie #15513 (England) is an edition of 20,000 dolls exclusive to Hamleys of London, "the Finest Toyshop in the World." She wears a white sweatshirt with the Hamleys logo, red leggings, black boots, and a Hamleys hat. She carries a Hamleys shopping bag. $25.00.

1997 Boutique Barbie #19020 (England) wears a pink sweater with a pastel-print collar, cuffs, and headband with a denim skirt and white belt. She carries a shopping bag featuring the "B" logo. $20.00.

1997 Princess Sissy #18058 was released to complement the U.S. Empress Sissy Barbie. Princess Sissy uses the SuperStar Barbie head mold with brown eyes and thigh-length straight brown hair. She wears a magnificent gold gown with white satin ribbon trim, a white satin underskirt, and glittery tulle. A dazzling choker, golden earrings, gold pumps, and a shiny golden tiara complete her ensemble. Her box back states, "Princess Sissy was a beautiful, kind girl, loved by everyone, destined to marry and become an Empress!" $40.00.

1997 Das Spielzeug Barbie (Austria) commemorates the fortieth anniversary of Austria's Pallendorf store in a limited edition of only 100 dolls wearing stylish two-piece suits featuring skirts, matching jackets with white satin lapels, white shells, short white gloves, white pearl necklaces and earrings, headbands in the color of the suit, and matching pumps. Each doll comes with a leather-look white purse, a doll stand, and a wrist tag labeled "fashion dreams by E. Stelzer Vienna" on the front with the doll's individual number on the back. Re-dressed Puerto Rican Barbie dolls from the DOTW series were used for this collection. $250.00 each.

1998 Chica Dehoy Ultima Geracao Marie #20968 (Spain, Portugal) is identical to the U.S. Generation Girl Lara, but she is called Marie in Spain and Portugal, and her box and booklet are printed in Spanish and Portugese. $45.00.

1998 Chica Dehoy Ultima Geracao Susie #20969 (Spain, Portugal) is identical to the U.S. Generation Girl Tori, but she is called Susie in Spain and Portugal, and her box and booklet are printed in Spanish and Portugese. $40.00.

1998 Children's Day Barbie #18350 wears a shiny striped bodice, pink satin skirt, and pink heart and stars necklace. She comes with two cardboard Barbie friendship bracelets. $15.00.

1998 Cool Sitter Baby-sitter Teen Skipper #20334 (England) comes with two Li'l Friends of Shelly dolls at a special price. $45.00.

1998 Fruit Fantasy Barbie #21386 wears a sparkly pink shirt with an iridescent pink strawberry-print skirt with a green satin ribbon accent. A bottle of strawberry fragrance and a strawberry necklace are included for the child. $20.00.

1998 Fruit Fantasy Barbie #20319 has brown hair and wears a sparkly peach shirt with an iridescent peach-print skirt with a green satin ribbon accent. A bottle of peach fragrance and a peach necklace are included for the child. Both Fruit Fantasy dolls use the Mackie head mold. $25.00.

1998 Li'l Friends of Shelly Cowgirl Chelsie #21639 has dark red hair, green eyes, and freckles. This deluxe edition includes a plastic rocking horse. $45.00.

1998 Li'l Friends of Shelly Playtime Jenny #21640 has black hair and brown eyes. Jenny wears denim overalls, a white t-shirt, and red shoes, and she pulls a wagon carrying a pail, a shovel, and a ball. $45.00.

1998 Pony Riding Shelly wears a horse-riding costume with cream pants, black shoes, a black riding hat, and a vest with attached white sleeves. Both green and blue vests have been found.

#19881, $18.00.

#23767, $24.00.

1998 Kastner & Ohler Barbie #9935-9041 (Austria) commemorates the 125th anniversary of Austria's Kastner & Ohler store, founded in 1873. Barbie doll, a re-dressed Chilean Barbie from the DOTW collection, wears a lovely late-nineteenth century fashion featuring an emerald top coat with striped lapels over a striped skirt. An emerald green hat with flowers and a parasol complement her costume. Her hang tag reads, "Fashion Dreams by E. Stelzer Vienna" on the front with the doll's individual number on the back. $395.00.

1998 Lisboa Expo '98 Barbie #18616 (Portugal) was created to commemorate Lisbon's Expo '98, which promoted the theme, "The Oceans, a Heritage for the future." Barbie doll wears an orange, yellow, and blue wetsuit and comes with sparkly flippers, a snorkel, oxygen tanks, and a dolphin. The cartoon mascot on the box front is Gil, who works with Barbie doll to keep our oceans clean. $45.00.

1999 Milan Barbie #24838 (Italy) uses the Generation Girl Barbie head mold. She wears a red and black soccer shirt featuring the logos of sponsors OPEL, Adidas, and ACM, white shorts with red stripes on the side, white knee-high socks with red bands, and sneakers. A soccer ball is included. Her box uses the logo "100 MILAN 1899 – 1999." $35.00.

1998 Riviera Barbie #22974 has stylish short hair and wears a floral-print blue sundress with blue pumps. $15.00.

1998 *Life Ball Barbie 98* (Austria) is an edition of 1,000 dolls by British designer Vivienne Westwood for the Life Ball AIDS charity event in Vienna, Austria. The doll is a Great Eras Victorian Lady Barbie with restyled hair re-dressed in a brown gown with a golden Vivienne Westwood tag at the waist. Her thigh-length golden earrings were designed by Laurent Rivaud. The doll cost $500.00 originally. $550.00.

1999 *Life Ball Barbie 99* (Austria) is an edition of 500 dolls designed by Christian LaCroix. The doll is a Rendezvous Barbie doll re-dressed in an orange gown with black trim. $575.00.

1999 *Barbie Style* #20766 wears a red floral-print dress with a black collar. She uses the Mackie head mold, but the same doll was sold in the U.S. using the SuperStar Barbie head mold. $15.00.

1999 Baumgarten Biedermeier Barbie is an extremely limited edition of 100 dolls commemorating the 170th anniversary of the Biedermeier store of Vienna, Austria, founded in 1829. She is a re-dressed Austrian Barbie wearing an early nineteenth century costume featuring a brown satin blouse with a pink rose on the bodice, a gold vest and skirt with pink bows on the skirt hem, and an elegant hat with ribbon. Her hangtag reads, "fashion dreams by E. Stelzer Vienna" on the front with the doll's individual number on the back. $450.00.

1999 Barbie Estate (Italy) packages the European Weekend Barbie with the SuperStar Barbie head mold wearing a pink t-shirt, short floral-print white overalls, and pink sneakers with an issue of Italy's *Barbie* magazine. $50.00.

1999 Blushing Bride Barbie #25776 uses the Generation Girl Barbie head mold. Her box back says, "'I do' is just a dream away for Barbie," indicating that Barbie doll's marrying is still just a dream. Her satin bridal gown shimmers with silvery touches and a tulle veil frames her face. She carries a bouquet of white roses. The same doll was sold as an Avon exclusive in different packaging in the U.S. in 2000. $35.00.

1999 Freunde Furs Leben Gratuliert Barbie #98142 (Germany) is an edition of only 1,500 sets packaging the 40th Anniversary Barbie with another time-less toy, the Steiff teddy bear, identical in design and color to the Steiff bear of 1959, the year of Barbie doll's debut. $225.00.

1999 Riviera Barbie #26219 has brown hair and blue eyes. She wears a simple yet stylish blue and white striped dress with blue open-toe heels. $20.00.

1999 Riviera Barbie #26220 has red hair and green eyes. She wears a pretty green, yellow, and white striped dress with green open-toe heels. A blonde Riviera Barbie wearing a striped purple version of this dress and her African-American counterpart were sold in the U.S. $20.00.

1999 Little Friend of Shelly Baker Chelsie #24610 has green eyes and freckles. She wears a pink and white gingham dress with white apron and pink shoes. She comes with a measuring cup, a mixing bowl, a whisk, a cookie sheet, and a spoon. $45.00.

1999 Little Friend of Shelly Biker Baby Jenny #24608 has dark brown hair and green eyes. Jenny wears a blue and white bandana on her head, a silver jacket, blue pants with pink cuffs, and blue sneakers. She comes with a plastic Big Wheels bike. $45.00.

1999 Little Friend of Shelly Li'l Swimmer Kayla #24609 wears a blue floral-print swimsuit and comes with beach accessories and a beach chair. $45.00. Courtesy of Katrina McDowell.

1999 Shelly & Thirsty Pony Gift Set #22881 includes Shelly wearing her riding costume with the green vest along with her pony that "drinks" the water that Shelley pumps. $55.00.

2000 Friend of Shelly Kitty Fun Melody #28049 wears a pink and white top featuring a white kitten-face decal, an attached pink floral-print skirt, and shoes. She comes with a plastic white cat and a cat bed. $40.00.

2000 Friend of Shelly Winter Fun Nikki #28047 wears a black and white houndstooth skirt, a red coat, a white scarf, sheer white stockings, and black shoes. She is packaged with a sled, a "snowball," and a tiny white bear. $50.00.

2000 Little Friend of Kelly Spring Cleaning Jenny #28048 wears denim over-alls, a blue dot-print shirt and matching headkerchief, and red shoes. She carries a bucket with a purple cleaning rag and is packaged with a toy vacuum cleaner. $60.00. Courtesy of Laurel Willoughby.

2000 Amusement Park Tamera #29201 is known as Nia in the U.S. $28.00. Courtesy of Laurel Willoughby.

2000 Chic Barbie #50565 wears a pink dress and molded-on slippers. $15.00.

2000 Happy Birthday Barbie #50506 wears a lavender party dress with blue floral designs on the skirt and satin ribbons at the waist. She comes with a plastic birthday cake, a party hat, a gift box, an invitation, and ankle-strap pumps. $28.00.

2000 Party Barbie #29011 wears a pink satin party dress and molded-on pink slippers. She is packaged with a porcelain-look tea service. $20.00.

2000 Photographer Ken #29903 features Ken doll with rooted brown hair and blue eyes. He wears khaki shorts, a red shirt with a white stripe, and black sneakers. He holds a 35mm camera that has a simulated flash and a plastic camera bag. Three pictures "develop" when exposed to warm water in his developing tray. A plastic dog with a red satchel and a bone, and a telephoto lens is included. $30.00.

2000 Shelly Club Shelly #29837 is identical to the Pet Lovin' Puppy Twins and Kelly set sold in the U.S. at Target stores, but this European Shelly is packaged without the puppies. $45.00. Courtesy of Katrina McDowell.

2000 Sydney 2000 Olympic Fan Barbie is a collection of 10 dolls wearing Olympic workout uniforms with matching jackets and white sneakers. Barbie uses the Generation Girl Barbie head mold with strawberry blonde hair, blue eyes, and red lips, and she carries the cardboard flag of each of the 10 countries she represents. A gold medal is included with each doll. $25.00 each.

Australia #25975

Canada #25974

Brazil #25980

France #25976

Greece #25977

Germany #25961

Italy #25982

Spain #25979

Mexico #26052

Puerto Rico #26053

Barbie 131

2000 Velina Barbie (Italy) includes Barbie doll with the Generation Girl Barbie head mold with blonde hair and brown eyes. She wears a pink "VELINA" t-shirt, floral-print shorts, and sneakers. She is packaged with an issue of Italy's *Barbie* magazine that features Velina Barbie on the cover. $50.00.

2001 Barbie Princess Gift Set #52777 (England) includes blonde Barbie doll wearing a pink skirt with a sheer pink illusion bodice with a white satin midriff panel featuring silver threading, a metallic silver tiara, and a metallic silver necklace featuring the "B" logo pendant. Three additional elegant gowns with purses, shoes, tiaras, and jewelry are included. $50.00.

2001 Birthday Barbie #52640 wears a pink party dress with overskirt. A plastic birthday cake with four candles, a gift box, and a faux pearl strand necklace for the child is included. $30.00.

2001 Ballerina Maura #52841 is identical to the Ballerina Lorena sold in the U.S., but Lorena is called Maura in Europe. $15.00.

2001 Camper Susie #53469 is identical to the Camper Marisa sold in the U.S., but Marisa is called Susie in Europe. $15.00.

2001 Day in the Sun Brunette Barbie #29389 (France) is an edition of 1,100 brunette dolls created for the Paris Fashion Doll Festival and the cancelled Chicago Fashion Doll Festival; the regular version is blonde. Each of the two events was supposed to receive 550 brunette dolls, but when the Chicago event was cancelled, those 550 dolls were sold through the Barbie Collector's Club. The Paris Fashion Doll Festival dolls have gold "Paris Fashion Doll Festival" stickers on their box windows. She wears a leopard-print swimsuit with a black chiffon sarong, platform sandals, a wide-brim straw weave hat with sheer black scarf, sunglasses, and bracelets. $75.00.

2001 Hot Wheels Racing Michael Schumacher Collection (France) wears a racing uniform matching the American Scuderia Ferrari Barbie doll's. His box states, "In honor of one of the most exciting and successful Formula One drivers of our era, HOT WHEELS Racing has produced a limited edition 30.48 cm figure of three-time World Champion Michael Schumacher. This highly detailed collectible figure is clad in official team colors, helmet, and authentic race suit with sponsors' logos." His head is sculpted in Schumacher's likeness. $75.00.

2001 Style Boulevard Barbie #55687 boasts five mix 'n match looks. $24.00.

2002 Chic Barbie #56805 is a basic Barbie doll using the Generation Girl Barbie head mold with blonde shoulder-length hair parted on her left, blue eyes, and red lips. She wears a cocktail dress with metallic accents and red pumps, and she carries a cardboard purse. $20.00 each.

2002 Cinderella Barbie #61316 has strawberry blonde hair and violet eyes. She wears a lavender ball gown with sparkly sheer purple overskirt panels, a satin bodice with purple floral designs and sparkly sheer purple sleeves, and a lavender tiara. Glittery "glass" pumps are included. Her box back states, "When the prince found her lost glass slipper after the ball, he helped make her dream come true!" $40.00.

2002 Princess & the Pea Barbie #61314 has brown hair and green eyes. She wears a turquoise satin gown featuring a central floral-print ice blue panel on the bodice and the skirt and a gold tiara. She comes with a cardboard pillow holding a pea. Her box back says, "Only a true princess can feel a pea under many mattresses, said the queen. When one girl did, the prince happily married her." $40.00.

2002 Snow White Barbie #56035 has black hair, pale skin, blue eyes, and red lips. She wears a blue gown featuring a blue bodice with white floral print, a blue skirt with a sheer blue overskirt, and a white faux fur jacket with sheer blue sleeves. A pearl necklace and a blue tiara complete her ensemble. $45.00.

2002 Flower Surprise Ken #56781 (England, Australia) has rooted brown hair and blue eyes. He wears a dashing black tuxedo with a pink bow tie and pink cummerbund. He carries a realistic box of chocolate candy and a bouquet of cloth flowers for Barbie doll. His handkerchief transforms into a corsage. $30.00.

2002 *Horse Lovin' Barbie #61317* has platinum blonde hair and violet eyes, and she uses the bend and move body. $30.00.

2002 *My Scene Westley #62231*. In Europe Barbie doll's American African-American friend Madison is called Westley. $25.00.

2002 *Polinesia Barbie #138* (Italy) is a special promotional doll for Italy's *Barbie* magazine. Polinesia Barbie wears a gold one-piece swimsuit with a sheer rose wrap skirt. She is packaged with the August 2002 issue #138 of *Barbie* magazine. Note that Polinesia Barbie is featured on the magazine cover. $50.00.

2002 *Wedding Day Barbie #60290* has blue-green eyes. She has three different looks for the "day of her dreams." Her gown changes for the ceremony, the reception, and the honeymoon. $30.00.

2003 Barbie As Mermaid Princess #c5540 has auburn waist-length hair parted on her right and blue eyes. She wears a mermaid costume featuring an iridescent white top, a shimmering purple mermaid skirt with ocean blue sheer glittery panels that match her detached sleeves, and an oyster-shell blue headpiece. A fish-shaped comb and bonus accessories are included. $36.00.

2003 Ken as Fairytale Prince #c4900 has rooted blond hair and blue eyes. He wears a satiny white shirt with silver braid trim, dusty blue trousers, gray boots, and a silver crown. $40.00.

2003 Barbie Estate #150 (Italy) wears a two-piece pink floral-print swimsuit with orange trim and orange sunglasses. A beach bag is included. She is a promotional doll packaged with Italy's Barbie magazine issue #150. $45.00.

2003 Gay Parisienne Barbie #B2366 (France) is a limited edition of 300 blonde dolls created for the 2003 Paris Fashion Doll Festival. Her box lid has an illustration of the blonde Gay Parisienne Barbie and has the Paris Fashion Doll Festival Eiffel Tower logo and the words, "Paris Fashion Doll Festival March 2003." $200.00.

2003 Pet Pals Cheetah Tabitha #b5798 wears a leopard-print top with orange velour pants and gold sandals. She carries a plastic cheetah. Tabitha is known as Tamika in the U.S. $25.00.

2003 Sweetsville Tabitha #b5800 features a new "TOON LOOK." The same doll was sold in the U.S. as Sweetsville Tamika. $20.00.

2004 Barbie as Beauty #g8426 uses the enlarged Generation Girl Barbie head with brown hair parted on her right and blue eyes. She has blue legs and wears a blue ballet costume with a satiny blue floral-print bodice and a glittery blue tulle skirt, blue slippers, and a blue tiara. Her box back states, "You're invited to a very special ballet… The performance stars the most beautiful ballerina in the kingdom — the Barbie princess!" $26.00.

2004 Barbie as Snow White #g8427 uses the enlarged Generation Girl Barbie head with black hair parted on her left and violet eyes. She has lavender legs and wears a purple ballet costume with a satiny purple floral-print bodice and a glittery purple tulle skirt, purple slippers, and a purple tiara. $30.00.

2004 Barbie as Mermaid Princess #h3712 features Barbie with auburn hair and a purple clamshell crown. She wears an iridescent top with a shimmering purple mermaid's tail with sparkly sheer side panels. Bonus hair and jewelry accessories for Barbie doll and a lovely purple heart pendant set in silver is included for the child. $30.00.

2004 Barbie as Mermaid Princess Gift Set #g4013 includes Barbie with dark brown hair that turns purple when cold water is applied. She wears a mermaid costume with a shimmering removable cloth mermaid tail, a pearl necklace, and a clamshell crown. She comes with an extra blue satin blouse with striped skirt and a purple armoire filled with beauty accessories. $40.00.

2004 Barbie as Sleeping Beauty Gift Set #g4012 includes Barbie with light brown hair that turns pink when cold water is applied. She wears a blue satin gown and a blue crown, and she comes with an additional ball gown and a pink armoire filled with beauty accessories. $40.00.

2004 Enchanted Ball Prince Ken #g8428 has rooted brown hair and brown eyes. He wears a royal blue shirt with silver trim, a silver crown, gray pants, and gray boots. $28.00.

2004 Color Magic Barbie #C3830 (France) is a limited edition of 300 redheaded dolls produced for the 2004 Paris Fashion Doll Festival. The Paris Fashion Doll Festival logo with the Eiffel Tower icon appears on the box lid. $210.00.

2004 Ferrari Fashion Show Barbie #b9210 (England) uses the enlarged Generation Girl Barbie head with straight blonde hair parted on her left. She wears a white t-shirt featuring the Ferrari logo in red, denim bell-bottom jeans worn with a pink belt and silver buckle, a red jacket, a sheer blue scarf, shoes, and blue sunglasses. She carries a red tote and comes with a plastic red Ferrari suitcase on wheels. $35.00.

2004 Fiori Di Primavera Shelly #b6906 (Italy) features Shelly with the large "Toon" look head wearing a purple and white gingham dress accented by a rose on a yellow waistband and yellow sandals. She holds a purple gardening shovel and a yellow watering can, and she comes with three cardboard purple flower pots. She is packaged with the April 2004 Italian Barbie magazine. $100.00.

2004 Stella Marina Barbie #b6421 (Italy) has green eyes, freckles, and brown streaks in her blonde hair. She wears an orange floral-print swimsuit and comes with a star-shaped flotation ring. $35.00.

2004 Wiener Opernball Barbie (Austria) is a souvenir doll for attendees of Barbie doll's 45th anniversary celebration held at the Vienna Art Center in Austria on November 15, 2003. The doll's interior box lid states that Barbie turns 45 on February 19, 2004, and a "Die Barbie Story 45 Jahre" pamphlet is included. Note the box lid photo showing Barbie doll in front of the Vienna Art Center. $95.00.

2005 Barbie as Cinderella Giftset #j1006 includes Barbie and baby sister Shelly wearing matching pink and gold princess gowns with pink tiaras. Barbie has a pink mask for the ball. $40.00.

2005 Barbie as Cinderella Wedding Gift Set #h7451 includes blonde Barbie doll wearing a white satin gown with a gold collar, gold-trimmed satin ribbons, and gold patterns. A sheer white overskirt, a white tulle veil with a golden tiara, a gold necklace, earrings, golden pumps, and a white floral bouquet complete her bridal ensemble. Prince Ken has rooted brown hair and wears a golden crown, a purple jacket with gold braid trim, a vest with golden buttons over a white shirt, white pants, white stockings, and black dress shoes. Ken carries a pillow to which two wedding rings are sewn. A three-layer wedding cake featuring a heart-shaped cake topper containing a photo of Cinderella Barbie and Prince Ken, two goblets, a knife, and a cake server are included. The box states, "In a magnificent wedding gown, Barbie as Cinderella marries the prince. The two rings promise everlasting love!" $65.00.

2005 Barbie as Sleeping Beauty uses the enlarged Generation Girl Barbie head with a simulated bodice of glued-on glitter and legs molded in the color of her tulle skirt, an iridescent petal overskirt with a braid belt, a tiara, and color-coordinated slippers. $22.00 each.

#J0987

#J0988

#J0989

2005 Benetton Helsinki Barbie #j6256 has dark brown streaks in her blonde hair. She wears a black "Barbie" logo t-shirt, a sparkly pink jacket, a pink skirt with pink sequined belt, pink knee-high socks, and black boots. She comes with an additional fashion: a silver lamé top, belted denim capris, a sparkly black scarf, and silver shoes. She was only sold during the 2005 holiday season. $80.00.

2005 Benetton London Barbie #j2252 uses the Lea head mold. She wears a white shirt with a red "BENETTON" vest, a blue "65" miniskirt, a brown "leather" jacket with faux fur trim, striped blue knee-high socks, and boots. $30.00.

2005 Benetton New York Barbie #j2254 uses the Desiree head mold. She wears a striped shirt, a pink faux fur vest, belted denim capris, orange leggings, and sneakers. $38.00.

2005 Benetton Paris Barbie #j2253 uses the Lara head mold. She wears a gray "BENETTON" tank top with a pink shrug, a pink plaid miniskirt with pink belt, a pink scarf with brooch, pink pantyhose, and pink pumps. $36.00.

2005 Benetton Stockholm Barbie #j2251 uses the Mackie head mold. She wears a colorful patterned sweater, a white miniskirt, white leggings with pink snowflake designs, a striped scarf, a matching hat, and white boots. $30.00.

2005 Benetton Melbourne Barbie #j7883 uses the Cali Girl Summer head mold. She wears a blue and pink "BENETTON" shirt, a green terry jacket, a white skort, blue and pink leggings, and white sneakers. $40.00.

2005 Benetton Osaka Barbie #j7881 has the Lea head mold with pink streaks in her black hair, held by beads in two pigtails. She wears a blue "BENETTON" shirt with detached pink sleeves, an orange vest, blue and yellow striped capris, a denim miniskirt, and pink sneakers. $45.00.

2005 Girls Aloud Fashion Fever Barbie #j5478 was designed by Sarah Harding of the British pop singers Girls Aloud. The five-member Girls Aloud singing group formed in late 2002 on the British television program *Popstars: The Rivals*, and they made history as the first all-female group to debut in the number one spot for CD sales in the U.K. Barbie has the Cali Girl Summer head mold and wears a red jacket with black trim, gold buttons, and iridescent white waist panels and cuffs, along with black satin capris, a black belt, and black boots. $40.00.

2005 Girls Aloud Fashion Fever Courtney #j5477 is the creation of Nicola Roberts. She uses the Goddess of Africa head mold and wears a white dress with iridescent highlights and a silver floral clasp, a white shrug, and white shoes. $45.00.

2005 Girls Aloud Fashion Fever Drew #j5905 was designed by Nadine Coyle. Drew uses the Lara head mold with streaked brown hair. She wears a sparkling black top with silver trim, satiny white capris, black sunglasses, a pearl necklace and bracelet, and black shoes. $45.00.

2005 Girls Aloud Fashion Fever Kayla #j5479 is Kimberley Walsh's entry in the collection. Kayla uses the Lea head mold. She wears a white skirt with silver trim, a white sleeveless top with silver accents, a black belt with silver studs, two necklaces, a silver bracelet, hoop earrings, and white boots with black trim. $50.00.

2005 Girls Aloud Fashion Fever Teresa #j5476 is the product of Cheryl Tweedy Cole. Teresa wears a metallic pink and silver tank top, cuffed black denim jeans, a black belt with gray buckle, a white "leather" jacket, and black boots. $45.00.

2005 Evening Splendor Brunette Barbie #H8149 (France) is a Platinum Label brunette doll created for the Paris Fashion Doll Festival held March 18 – 20, 2005. Only 300 brunette dolls were created as a brunette version of the Gold Label blonde Evening Splendor Barbie. She wears a gold and white sheath dress with a matching gold coat with brown faux fur cuffs, a pearl necklace and earrings, short white gloves, and a brown faux fur hat with pearl accents. A turquoise purse, a hanky, and brown open-toe heels complete her ensemble. $175.00.

2005 Life Ball Barbie 2005 (Austria) is an edition of only 300 dolls designed by Valentino. Julia Roberts wore a life-size version of this dress at the 2001 Academy Awards when she received the Oscar for best actress. Barbie has the Mackie face with red lips, brown eyes, and dark brown hair with auburn highlights, and her gown has the "VALENTINO COUTURE" label. Her jewelry was designed by Ugo Cacciatori and is made of 925 precious sterling silver crystals supplied by Swarovski. Her box back states, "Life Ball is one of the most significant charity events in the fight against AIDS world wide. Besides the raising of the utmost possible financial means for people affected by AIDS/HIV, Life Ball is also concerned with creating awareness.. Since 1998, Life Ball, in co-operation with Mattel Inc., produces the strictly limited Life Ball Barbie in irregular periods." $600.00.

2005 Princess Collection Shelly as Cinderella #h9802 features Shelly wearing a pink princess gown with a pink tiara. She carries a hand mirror. $20.00.

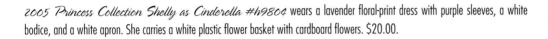

2005 Princess Collection Shelly as Cinderella #h9803 finds Shelly wearing a regal white satin gown with gold glitter accents and a gold tiara. She carries a single white rose. $20.00.

2005 Princess Collection Shelly as Cinderella #h9804 wears a lavender floral-print dress with purple sleeves, a white bodice, and a white apron. She carries a white plastic flower basket with cardboard flowers. $20.00.

2005 Shelly Tenera Amica #98bdo (Italy) features Shelly with the classic small Shelly/Kelly head mold with light blonde hair. She wears a long pink dress with pink shoes. She comes with an adorable brown plastic puppy dog, and holds a cardboard picture album with the name "Fido" on the cover. She is packaged with the April 2005 Italian *Barbie* magazine. $150.00.

2006 Benetton Capri Barbie #k5354 wears a pink "Wave Ride" hooded sweatshirt, pink sunglasses, a yellow UNITED COLORS OF BENETTON tank top with striped waistband, denim shorts with a pink belt, and sandals. A digital camera, a cell phone, a vinyl tote bag, and a suitcase are included. $35.00.

2006 Benetton Beijing Barbie #k5355 is Benetton Boutique's second holiday exclusive Barbie doll. She uses the Goddess of Africa head mold. She wears a rose satin shirt under a pink knit sweater and cranberry velveteen capris and navy blue shoes. A cranberry velveteen jacket, a denim miniskirt with pink ruffle, and a blue cloth handbag are included. $40.00.

2006 Benetton Berlin Barbie #k5602 uses the Lea head mold. She wears a pink "Rock Chick" Barbie guitar t-shirt, olive corduroy pants, a denim miniskirt, a purple hooded jacket with faux fur collar, a raspberry and purple scarf with fringe, pink socks, and sneakers. $36.00.

2006 Benetton Milan Barbie #k5603 uses the Lara head mold with a brown skin tone, brown eyes, and reddish-brown hair. She wears a camel-color jacket, a rust-color shirt, plaid knee-length pants with cuffs, a pink scarf, a matching pink cap, rust-color leggings, and pink boots. $30.00.

2006 Benetton Moscow Barbie #k5605 uses the Goddess of Africa head mold with fair skin tone, blonde hair, and brown eyes. She wears a green turtleneck with a brown corduroy skirt featuring two rows of flower designs, an ivory poncho with purple trim and floral appliqués, pink leggings, and brown boots. $35.00.

2006 Benetton St. Moritz Barbie #k5604 wears a white quilted coat with faux fur collar, a pink scarf, pink ski glasses, pink pants, faux fur leg warmers, and white boots. $25.00.

2006 Rhapsody in Paris Barbie #j9259 is a Platinum Label doll limited to only 200 dolls created for the Paris Fashion Doll Festival, held March 17 – 19, 2006. Barbie uses the Lea head mold with blonde hair, and she wears a turquoise blue taffeta version of the Barbie Fan Club's Rhapsody in New York brunette Barbie doll's purple gown. The gown wraps around one shoulder and is joined by a silver ring. Two tiers of large ruffles complete the dress, and a matching turquoise purse, pumps, and silver and turquoise drop earrings complete her ensemble. Her box lid features an illustration of this blonde doll, the Eiffel Tower, and the phrase, "Les Top Models a Paris Fashion Doll Festival 17, 18 et 19 Mars 2006." $300.00.

1986 Familie Herz Grobes Geschenkset! #5379 (Italy) includes the Heart Family Mom with her daughter wearing a matching costume along with a pink rocking horse and a Familie Herz booklet. Several styles, each repackaging an original mom and daughter, were available. $100.00 each.

1986 The Heart Family Box #3867 is a playpen with sliding beads. $20.00.

1986 The Heart Family New Arrival Baby Care Set #8389 (Italy) includes a white wicker-look rocking chair, a cot and stand, a nursery table, a pillow, a quilt, a nappy bucket, a baby bath, soap, a soap dish, a rattle, scales, two bottles, and two jars. $50.00.

1986 The Heart Family Tricycle #3868 (Italy) is "the twins' very own tricycle with detachable carrier." $25.00.

1987 The Heart Family Baby Wets #4661 includes Mom wearing a pink velvet dress with lacy white overskirt and white tulle collar, along with her baby boy wearing a striped blue suit with matching tie, attached pink shirt, and white stockings. A bottle and a box of diapers are included. The baby actually "drinks" from the bottle and wets his diaper. $75.00.

1987 The Heart Family Baby Wets #4662 includes Dad wearing a blue smoking jacket over white pants, a pink vest, and a blue scarf. His daughter wears a pink dress with white lace trim. $75.00.

1987 The Heart Family Futura Mamma Con Culla #4683 (Italy) features the Heart Family New Arrival Mom wearing a unique blue dress with white lace cuffs and lacy neck scarf, a blue maternity smock, her newborn baby wearing a white Christening gown, and a lace-covered cradle. $150.00.

1987 The Heart Family Rocking Horse #5110 includes a pink rocking horse, a yellow sleeper, and a cowboy hat. $30.00.

1987 The Heart Family Baby Fashions #5395 packages the ensemble worn by the American Baby Cousins Kevin and Highchair as a carded fashion in Europe. $25.00.

1987 The Heart Family Country Lace Dress #5256 is one of six Heart Family series Family Fashions produced exclusively for Europe. Interestingly, the baby fashions included in these six sets were available in the U.S. as carded Baby Fashions, so the Mom and Dad fashions were unique additions in Europe. $50.00.

1987, Nautical Outfit, #5265, Mom. $50.00.

1987, Nautical Outfit, #5267, Dad. $50.00.

1987, Robes, #5266, Mom. $50.00.

1987, Robes, #5274, Dad. $50.00.

1987, Springtime Flower Dress, #5260. $50.00.

1988 La Famille Doucoeur Playground Friends #3198 has blonde hair and blue eyes. He wears a cowboy fashion featuring a yellow shirt with a blue and white bandana and yellow and white striped cuffed pants. $50.00.

1988 La Famille Doucoeur Playground Friends #3203 has platinum blonde hair with a pink hair ribbon and blue eyes. She wears a blue floral-print dress with a white eyelet collar and hem and sheer white stockings. $50.00.

1988 *La Famille Doucoeur Playground Friends* #3206 has red hair, green eyes, and freckles. She wears a sleeveless white sailor dress with blue stars and a yellow bib collar featuring sparkling silver stars, white leggings, and a white sailor hat with blue stars on the brim. $50.00.

1988 *La Famille Doucoeur Playground Friends* #3210 has brown hair and blue eyes. He wears a sleeveless bodysuit featuring yellow shorts and an attached white shirt with blue stars and a red bib collar with a sparkling silver star, along with a white sailor hat with blue stars on the brim. $50.00.

1988 *La Famille Doucoeur Schooltime Fun* #2814 wears a pale pink short jumpsuit with a floral-print pink skirt, a pink jacket with an apple "ABC" appliqué, and blue heart-rim eyeglasses. Her toddler boy wears blue and white striped overalls with a matching bowtie, a yellow jumpsuit, and a cap. Teacher Mom uses stencils, a plastic ruler, a plastic pencil, and plastic scissors to teach. At gym time Teacher Mom sheds her jacket and skirt and the boy sheds his overalls for hopscotch and soccer. A plastic thermos is included for lunchtime. $90.00.

1988 *The Heart Family Girl & Tricycle* #2076 is a Caucasian version of the African-American Tawny and Trike sold in the U.S. The doll's fashion, tricycle, wagon, and hair ribbon are identical in both sets; only the doll's race has been changed. $75.00.

1989 La Famille Doucoeur Baby Wets & Potty Chair #9046 includes a brown-haired girl with blue eyes and a blue hair ribbon wearing a blue floral-print playsuit with a white bib collar accented by a blue bow. A box of diapers, a bottle, blue shoes, and a potty chair are included. $60.00.

1989 La Famille Doucoeur Kindergarten Friends #4801. $50.00.

1989 La Famille Doucoeur Kindergarten Friends #4802 has blonde hair and blue eyes. She wears a pink skirt with white leggings, a white sweater with pink collar and floral appliqué, and a pink hat. $50.00.

1989 La Famille Doucoeur Kindergarten Friends #4804 has red hair, blue eyes, and freckles. She wears a yellow vinyl raincoat with pink and blue hearts, a pink collar, and a matching hat. $50.00.

1989 La Famille Doucoeur Kindergarten Friends #4805 has brown hair and blue eyes. She wears blue overalls with a white shirt with blue dots. $50.00.

1989 *La Famille Doucoeur Visits Disneyland Musical Carousel* is a rotating carousel that hold four children. The four vehicles feature illustrations of Disney characters, and music plays as the carousel turns. $85.00.

1989 *La Famille Doucoeur Visits Disneyland Musical Dumbo #2942* is a wind-up Dumbo ride that features Dumbo moving forward and backward as music plays. $65.00.

2002 Going Home Barbie 1st Edition is a special souvenir doll created by Mattel Hong Kong as a gift to adopting parents staying at the White Swan Hotel in Guangzhou, China. Barbie wears a pink dress with a blue floral-print bodice. Her Chinese baby has black hair and brown eyes and wears a romper with a white bib featuring two bears. The box front states, "For ages 14 and over" and "This is not a toy," and the box back states, "This souvenir is presented by Mattel (HK) Ltd to adopting parents of Chinese orphan children staying at the White Swan Hotel, Guangzhou, China." Since the doll was not offered for sale in stores and was only given to adopting parents staying at the White Swan Hotel, the doll is very rare, especially since most new parents wish to keep the doll as a souvenir of the adoption. Each Barbie doll is this series uses the Generation Girl Barbie head mold. $400.00.

2003 Going Home Barbie 2nd Edition wears the lavender sweater and blue scarf from the 2001 "Concert on the Green" Fashion Avenue, along with light blue floral-print capri pants. Her Chinese baby wears a pink romper with white dots and a brown bear-face bib. $300.00.

2004 Going Home Barbie 3rd Edition has strawberry blonde hair and wears an off-the-shoulders blue blouse with pink floral print, a tan "suede" skirt decorated with purple flowers, and a tan "suede" hat. Her Chinese baby wears a playsuit with a yellow and white gingham top and white shorts with blue and green floral designs. $285.00.

2005 Going Home Barbie 4th Edition has strawberry blonde hair worn with a single braid. She wears a sleeveless white pastel-print dress with a ruffle at the hem, a peach net shrug with matching cap and peach platform sandals. Her adopted infant wears a yellow playsuit with a brown and blue diamond-print pattern. Her box states that she is the "4th Edition of a Continuing Series." $240.00.

2006 Going Home Barbie 5th Edition has blonde hair with dark blonde streaks. She wears a knit top with a tiered blue skirt with fringe, a matching jacket with a single lavender flower, a blue hat, and blue platform shoes. Her Chinese baby wears a white bodysuit with a multi-color striped skirt. $175.00.

2006 Going Home Barbie 5th Edition wears a variant black dress with jacket and hat. Barbie has streaked blonde hair and violet eyes. Her box back states that she is the "5th Edition of a Continuing Series" and notes, "This souvenir is presented by Mattel (HK) Ltd. to adopting parents of Chinese orphan children staying at the White Swan Hotel, Guangzhou, China." $225.00.

Hong Kong

1996 Sweet Moments Barbie Gift Set #64341 wears a pink and white gingham dress decorated with a daisy on the bodice over a white t-shirt. She is packaged with a pink child-size Barbie backpack, a real watch, and a music CD. $65.00.

1997 Hong Kong Commemorative Edition Chinese Empress Barbie #16708 commemorates the return of Hong Kong's sovereignty to China in July 1997. The set includes Chinese Empress Barbie, a commemorative gold coin bearing the doll's likeness, a Barbie Collectibles drawstring coin pouch, and a numbered certificate of authenticity. $95.00.

1998 Hong Kong Anniversary Edition Golden Qi-Pao Barbie #20649 commemorates the July 1998 first anniversary of Hong Kong's reunification with China. This set, limited to 8,888 sets, contains Golden Qi-Pao Barbie, a commemorative gold coin bearing the doll's likeness, a coin pouch, a numbered certificate of authenticity, and a Qi-Pao Story booklet. The booklet states, "To celebrate the 1st anniversary of Hong Kong's reunification with China, Barbie models a fabulous Qi-Pao or cheon sam, portraying an ambassadress of the Orient. With this special Golden Qi-Pao Barbie doll, she shows us just how to combine Eastern charm with Western glamour." $80.00.

1989 Dreamtime Barbie #9180 wears a lavender nightgown with a sheer lavender floral-print peignoir and lavender pumps. She carries her plush pink teddy bear, B.B., which has a silver bow around its neck. The doll is nearly identical to her American counterpart except the Indian version has harsher makeup and her back is imprinted, "c MATTEL, INC. 1987 INDIA." Note the LEO Mattel symbol on the lower box front. $35.00.

1990 Wedding Fantasy Barbie #9916 is a lovely blonde bride with blue eyes. She wears a white satin wedding gown featuring a sheer white overskirt with white lace designs and a lace-trimmed neckline, a white floral headdress, and white pumps. She carries a bouquet of plastic flowers. As an introductory offer, a free "DESIGNER NIGHT GOWN" is included. $95.00.

1991 Teacher Barbie Presentation Set #9912 includes Barbie wearing a navy blue skirt with a blue vest and a pale pink blouse. The "Teacher Changes to Breathtaking Beauty," according to the box, when she changes into her dotted pink skirt with sleeveless white bodice. A plastic blackboard, pumps, and school supplies are included. $75.00.

1991 School-Going Skipper #1284 uses the 1985 Hot Stuff Skipper head mold with blonde hair worn with bangs and two satin ribbons. She wears a blue jumper dress school uniform featuring a flower sticker crest over a white shirt with a red necktie. An extra play costume, an "I LOVE SCHOOL" vinyl book bag, plastic school accessories, and shoes are included. $65.00.

1991 - 1992 Barbie in India #9910 dolls are dressed in all-seasons' classic sarees with exotic borders. Gold metal earrings, a handring, bangle bracelets, and a necklace with a red "jewel" complement the authentic fashions, which are worn with blouses and open-toe heels. The box states, "Barbie looks ravishing in her Indian clothes! A new dimension to dressing magnificence...Barbie is totally at home in India! A unique give and take of two cultures!" Each doll in the ongoing Barbie in India series uses the SuperStar Barbie head mold. From 1991 to mid-1993 the dolls were sold in slim boxes with green box liners covered with white stars. Barbie has a red Hindu circle or teardrop dot on her forehead. In launching this series, Mattel Leo claimed, "In India, Barbie has chosen some pretty special clothes that look stunning. There is a superb choice of outfits in rich jewel colors coordinated in romantic brocades; also silky easy-care fabrics — all perfect ingredients of Barbie's special occasion styles. Barbie is all set to steal the show!" Indeed, the Mattel Leo 1992 retailer catalog reported that Barbie in India received the Doll of the Year award! $45.00 each.

1992 My Best Friend Barbie is a basic, inexpensive Barbie doll. She wears a purple turtleneck blouse with a floral-print skirt and pumps. $35.00.

1992 School-Going Skipper #1284 wears a blue jumper dress with a white shirt and a red tie and a yellow school crest featuring a flower. She uses the closed-mouth Skipper head mold and has white satin ribbons in her hair. She has one extra fashion and comes with a vinyl "I LOVE SCHOOL" school bag, a water bottle, a pencil box, a lunch box, a writing board, and a comb. The photo on the box back shows this Skipper with the Hot Stuff Skipper head. Her box says, "Skipper comes from school and changes into her play clothes!" $60.00.

India

1992 Happy Birthday Barbie #9915 has a lovely complexion and pale blonde hair. She wears her most extravagant birthday gown featuring a pale pink bodice with poufy confetti-print sleeves, a white "Happy Birthday" satin sash, and a long pink skirt with sheer overskirt adorned with confetti, hearts, and sparkle designs. $30.00.

1995, #9919

1992 Barbie in Office includes Barbie doll's blue business suit featuring a blue skirt, a matching jacket with white lapels, a white shell, a white hat, white pumps, a white briefcase, a white purse, a calculator, and "THE TIMES OF INDIA" newspaper with the headline "PM reviews state of economy." $25.00.

1995

1995, #9910

1995, #9917

1993 - 1994 Barbie in India #9910 is sold in a wider box with a wrap-around window with a "FREE GIFT INSIDE!" notice in the top right corner of the box. The same sari styles and color combinations and jewelry suites are reused in this series, although Barbie doll now has a softer complexion, and the blondes have lighter blonde hair. A new sari style introduced in 1993 features a sheer blouse with matching pants, a lined print skirt with matching scarf, and open-toe heels. The free gift is simply a cardboard Barbie photo frame featuring a photo of one blonde and two brunette Barbie in India dolls gathering flowers. $45.00 each.

1995, #9927, $45.00.

1996, #9928, $45.00.

1996, #9928, $45.00.

Courtesy of Colleen Spengler.

1996, #9929, $45.00.

1996, #9930,
$45.00.

1997, #9931,
$45.00.

1997, #9932,
$45.00.

1997, #9932,
$45.00.

1997, #9932, $45.00.

1995 Fairy Fantasy Skipper #1285 is "making happy wishes come true" in her fairy costume. She comes with a magic wand, and hooks and string enable her to simulate flying. "The Fairy Fantasy Skipper Story" inside the box tells of Fairy Flora initiating Skipper as a fairy. $65.00.

1995 Flight Time Barbie #1115 wears a blue pilot's suit with a blue bowtie and a blue hat. An apron transforms her into an air hostess. A vanity case, a passport, a travel guide, a magazine, and blue pumps are included. A wings brooch is included for the child. $55.00.

1995 Paint 'N Dazzle Barbie wears a shiny gold bodice, a black skirt, a black jacket, and gold hoop earrings. She is packaged with fabric paint, sequins, garnets, rosettes, and rhinestones to decorate her costume and her skin. $35.00.

1995 Pretty Hair Barbie #1112 has "the longest hair ever" with her ankle-length brown hair. She wears an orange dress with black waist wrap, an orange hair decoration, and gold hoop earrings. Each Pretty Hair Barbie doll comes with Barbie Styling Gel, five hair accessories, pumps, and a hair styling booklet. $35.00.

1995 *Pretty Hair Barbie #1112* has ankle-length brown hair. She wears a green dress with black waist wrap, a green hair decoration, and gold hoop earrings. $35.00.

1995 *Pretty Hair Barbie #1112* has ankle-length blonde hair. She wears a pink confetti-print dress with a pink hair decoration and pink earrings. $35.00.

1995 *School-Going Skipper #1284* wears a red jumper school uniform dress with a white shirt and a blue tie. Her school crest still features a single flower. She comes with a different extra costume, along with a water bottle, shoes, a school bag, a pencil box, a lunch box, a writing board, and a comb. Her box back shows this new closed-mouth Skipper wearing the red school uniform. $65.00.

1995 *My First Barbie #1875* wears a white dress with white lace trim and a pink satin waist band, and her hair is accented with a pink hair bow. Her box states that she is "So Pretty, So Charming and So Easy To Dress." $30.00.

1995 My First Barbie #1788 is the doll with "shiny, smooth legs that slide easily into skirts, dresses, or pants" and "straight arms that slip easily into clothes." She wears a pink ballerina costume with a skirt covered with silver bars. She has unusual eyebrows. $30.00.

1996 My First Princess Barbie #1121 has a gorgeous skin tone with delicate face paint. She wears a pretty blue princess dress with a satin bodice and a sheer blue collar with a gold and blue pendant, a blue overskirt decorated with satin bows, a golden crown with "jewel," and blue pumps. $35.00.

1996 My First Ken #9809 uses the 1983 Crystal Ken head mold with blue eyes. While the picture on his box shows Ken wearing contemporary jeans and a sweater, this doll actually wears traditional Indian attire: an ivory tunic with a brown vest. His box states, "Meet Ken! Ken is Barbie's best friend. You and Ken can become the best of pals, too! Ken is full of fun. How about having tons of fun with Ken?" $65.00.

1996 My First Skipper #9911 wears a pink heart-print dress with white lace collar. She uses the closed-mouth head mold. Her box reveals, "Skipper is Barbie's younger sister. Not only is she pretty but also has her own wardrobe. Barbie and Skipper have lots of fun together, they jog together, have tea parties, and more." The box cites her straight arms, shiny smooth legs, and easy-to-put-on fashions. $48.00.

1996 My First Skipper #9911 wears a white dress with multicolored stripes and a magenta bow on the bodice. $48.00.

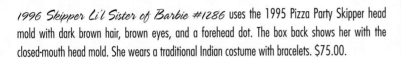

1996 Skipper Li'l Sister of Barbie #1286 uses the 1995 Pizza Party Skipper head mold with dark brown hair, brown eyes, and a forehead dot. The box back shows her with the closed-mouth head mold. She wears a traditional Indian costume with bracelets. $75.00.

1996 Li'l Friends of Barbie is a brunette blue-eyed girl wearing a green dress with white trim on the skirt. She uses the Heart Family baby head and body molds. The box backs on the two Li'l Friends of Barbie inexplicably show the Kelly/Shelly friends Becky, Chelsie, and Melody instead of these toddlers. $65.00.

1996 Li'l Friends of Barbie is a brown-eyed brown-haired boy wearing red plaid shorts with an attached white shirt and suspenders. The boy uses the Heart Family baby body with the head created for the male student of the 1996 U.S. Teacher Barbie. $75.00.

1996 Happy Holidays Barbie #1682 wears a dramatic red gown in the same style as the Toys 'R' Us 1995 Purple Passion Barbie; the box back even features a full-length photo of Purple Passion Barbie in her purple gown instead of this Happy Holidays Barbie. Note the magnificent golden packaging with silver box liner. $100.00.

1997 Happy Holidays Barbie #1139 wears a black velvet dress with tiny white dots and red floral lace skirt panels, a red floral lace collar with a single flower at the bodice, and a black hat with a flower. She has a beauty mark above her lips. $80.00.

1996 Expressions of India Roopvati Rajasthani Barbie #34016 is the first doll in the Expressions of India four-doll collection. Each doll in this series uses the SuperStar Barbie head mold with black hair and brown eyes. She wears a magnificent beaded costume with golden earrings, a gold bead necklace, bracelets, a jeweled headdress, and a gold nose ring. $75.00.

1997 Expressions of India Sohni Punjab Di Barbie #9937 depicts Barbie doll from Punjab, "the great frontier land that lives in rhythm with the Bhangra beat and folk culture." Women in Punjab typically wear an embroidered full-sleeved kurta, lungi, and a jacket. Flashy jewelry, a diamond nose stud, and a pink circle forehead dot are framed by her long dark hair, braided with gold cord, and pink sandals complete her ensemble. $100.00.

1997 Expressions of India Mystical Manipuri Barbie #9934 has the SuperStar Barbie head with brown eyes and a forehead dot. Her costume is adorned with gold, and her bell-shaped dress features mirrors. $100.00.

1997 Expressions of India Swapna Sundari Barbie #9938 is dressed as a Bharat Natyan temple dancer from south India. She wears shimmering silk, bordered with gold thread and a double finely pleated fan-like appendage tucked into the center of the hip belt. The dancer has an elaborate plait entwined with jasmine. Dazzling temple jewelry adds opulence to her costume, and her unique headdress frames her forehead symbol and nose stud. $100.00.

1998 Wedding Fantasy Barbie & Ken #1682 are packaged together in left over 1997 Happy Holidays Barbie packaging; the box back still features the photo of Purple Passion Barbie instead of this wedding pair. $125.00.

1999 Barbie in India #9941 wears a white floral lace dress featuring a blue and gold pattern, a blue vest, an ankle-length blue skirt, blue bangle bracelets, gold jewelry, a sheer white scarf with blue trim, and blue open-toe heels. $130.00.

2000 Capri Cool Barbie #49117 wears blue capris with a striped shirt, matching hat, and green shoes. She carries a green heart-shape purse and comes with green sunglasses and a hand mirror. She uses the SuperStar Barbie head mold with unusual yellow/blue eyes. $30.00.

1999 Kelly Baby Sister of Barbie #5481 introduces Barbie doll's tiny sister to India. Her box back says, "Hi! My name is Kelly. I am Barbie's baby sister. Barbie is the best sister in the whole world. I have lots of friends. We play hide and seek, collect sea shells, and build castles in the sand. We have lots of fun together." Kelly has brown hair and brown eyes and wears an ivory dress with brown and red floral designs with white shoes. $75.00. Courtesy of Laurel Willoughby.

1999 Kelly Baby Sister of Barbie #5483 has reddish-blonde hair, brown eyes, and red lips. She wears a pink dress with white satin bands on her skirt and white shoes. $75.00. Courtesy of Laurel Willoughby.

2000 Kelly Baby Sister of Barbie #5489 has brown hair accented with pink satin bows, brown eyes, and red lips. She wears a yellow top with black collar, a black skirt with floral designs, and black shoes. A cloth purse is included. $75.00. Courtesy of Laurel Willoughby.

2000 Kelly Baby Sister of Barbie #5490 has blonde hair and blue eyes. She wears floral-print top with a red skirt, a matching cap, and red shoes. $65.00. Courtesy of Laurel Willoughby.

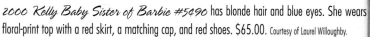

2000 Kelly Baby Sister of Barbie #6428 has blue eyes and red lips. Her box has a special sticker offering "free cute hairclips and win a trip to Disneyland Barbie Summer Magic Contest form inside pack." Kelly wears a red shirt, a yellow skirt with apples print, and red shoes. One pink hair clip and one blue hair clip for the child are included. $75.00.

2000 Kelly Baby Sister of Barbie #6484 has blue eyes and red lips and wears a blue dress featuring a white bodice, blue sleeves, and a single flower, and white shoes. A special offer includes free hairclips for the child and a Barbie Summer Magic Disneyland contest form. $75.00. Courtesy of Katrina McDowell.

2000 Kelly Li'l Sister of Barbie #5491 has brown eyes and blonde hair. She wears a blue and white dress featuring Hello Kitty illustrations. The sticker on her box advertises the Barbie Fashion Fever scratch 'n' win contest (a game card is inside the package), and a free tattoo and an iron-on sticker are included for the child. Note that Kelly is now called "Li'l Sister of Barbie," not "Baby Sister of Barbie." $65.00. Courtesy of Laurel Willoughby.

2000 Kelly Li'l Sister of Barbie #5495 has blonde hair and blue eyes. She wears a green shirt with a white collar, a white dress with red, green, and blue floral print, and white shoes. Her box also features the Barbie Fashion Fever contest sticker, free tattoo, and iron-on sticker. $65.00. Courtesy of Laurel Willoughby.

2000 Kelly Li'l Sister of Barbie #5498 has brown eyes and red lips and wears a black and white striped shirt with a yellow collar and a yellow skirt with yellow shoes. An iron-on sticker is included for the child. $20.00.

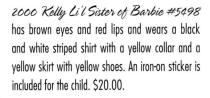

2000 Kelly Li'l Sister of Barbie #5500 has blue eyes and red lips and wears a block-print white dress with red shoes. An iron-on sticker is included for the child. $20.00.

2000 Festival Fun Barbie & Skipper #1156 features Barbie with the SuperStar Barbie head mold and little sister Skipper with the 1995 Pizza Party Skipper teenage head mold but original 1964 pre-teen body. Each doll has brown eyes, dark eyebrows, a red forehead dot, and dark brown hair. They wear elaborate festival costumes with ornate jewelry, golden headpieces, and pearl beading. $150.00.

2000 Wedding Fantasy Barbie #9940 uses the SuperStar Barbie head mold with brown eyes, a red forehead dot, and a golden nose stud on a chain connected to her headdress. She wears a magnificent rust-colored wedding gown with gold trim, and her layered skirts feature floral designs outlined in gold. Strands of gold beads circle her neck, and she wears numerous bracelets and elaborate gold earrings. This doll was reissued with the Generation Girl Barbie head mold with straight Shani arms in 2002 wearing this same dress and packaged in the same box. $85.00.

2001 Season's Special Barbie & Kelly includes the two sisters wearing matching red coats with white faux fur trim, along with a short, plush Santa Claus carrying a green bag of "gifts." $160.00.

2002 Barbie in India #49143 uses the Generation Girl Barbie head mold parted on her left, brown eyes, and a red forehead dot. Each doll wears gold ear- and bangle bracelets in one of four sari color combinations. $35.00 each.

2004 Expressions of India Roopvati Rajasthani Barbie #49140 is from the northwestern Indian state of Rajasthan, which means "land of the rajas," an area known for mystical deserts, royalty, and elaborate ceremonies. Barbie wears a multi-hued lehenga-choli (long skirt and bustier top) and dupatta (large stole) with sparkling zari work (gold and silver thread inlay) on vibrant bandhini (traditional tie and dye print). Colorful bangles, a shimmering maang-tika (head ornament), and a brilliant nose ring makes Barbie like a mirage in the desert. $65.00.

2004 Expressions f India Sundari Gujarati Barbie #49783 is from the vibrant state in west India renowned for its intricate arts and crafts and mirror work and handwork. Extravagant ceremonies mark Gujarati wedding festivities in a riot of color, tradition, and customs. Dressed in rich bridal colors, Sundari Gujarati Barbie doll glows in indescribable radiance. Her trousseau includes a pure silk 'Gharchola' (sari worn in traditional Gujarati style) with elegant zari (gold and silver thread inlay) work with a golden border. Her rustic jewelry is inlaid with stones, which look like mina (semi-precious gems). $65.00.

2004 Expressions of India Soni Punjabi Barbie #49784 is from Punjab, in north India, a land of warm and effervescent people who live out a rich tradition of food, folk music, and dance. A Punjabi wedding is well known all over India as perhaps the most joyous and festive of all. Soni Punjabi Barbie doll is dressed in a bright magenta salwar-kameez (drawstring pants worn under a knee-length tunic) typical to north India. This bridal outfit is unique to Punjab and is made of authentic raw silk fabric and decorated with an intricate floral pattern. A glittering sequined dupatta (head and shoulder wrap) discreetly covers her head in respect. An elaborate maang-tika (head-piece) and a fine Punjabi-style nose ring complements her beauty. $95.00.

2004 Expressions of India Wedding Fantasy Barbie #2125 is dressed as a bride in a beautiful traditional ghagra-choli (long skirt with bustier top) with zari work (gold and silver thread inlay) and Indian-styled bridal jewelry including a sparkling maang-tika (head ornament), splendid choker, colorful bangles, and shining nose ring. She has a bright red tika (crimson dot) on her forehead. $65.00.

2005 Indian Diva Barbie #g5230 uses the enlarged Generation Girl Barbie head. Her box back states, "Dressed in ethnic designer wear, Indian Diva Barbie doll is the life of any party. Oh, how heads turn to see such beauty in a chic kurta with a stylish capri and matching jooties!" Barbie is available in either a purple or a red kurta with gold lamé capris, a wrap, gold hoop earrings, and pointed-toe gold shoes. $35.00 each.

2006 Barbie in India #49143 is a series of six dolls using the Generation Girl Barbie head mold with brown eyes, a small red forehead dot, and straight black hair. Their box backs state, "Barbie is breathtakingly beautiful in her Indian avtaar. Dressed in colorful sarees, complete with bindi and ethnic jewelry, she's out to steal your heart. She symbolizes the values that are so intrinsic to any Indian. Truly, a picture of a traditional Indian beauty." Each doll wears a blouse with her sari, which features golden designs on the borders, a gold bead necklace, gold earrings, bangle bracelets, and sandals. $30.00 each.

1992 The Heart Family Mom & Baby #9078 wears a costume very similar to the American version, but the earliest Indian Heart Family Mom uses the Steffie head mold, while the American Mom has the 1979-dated Kelley (teen friend of Starr) head mold. This Indian Mom's eyes are turquoise, not blue like the American version, and her hair is more blonde than her American counterpart. The baby girl in both sets have minor differences. In India, the Heart Family is referred to as "Barbie's friends" and "Barbie's neighbors." $75.00.

1993 The Heart Family Mom & Baby #9078 was manufactured in 1993 with the Kelley head mold (the same as used by the American Mom), but the Indian doll's skin tone is much paler, her makeup is different, and her hair is a much lighter blonde. $35.00.

1992 The Heart Family Bunk Bed Playset #3866 includes a stackable pink bed for the girl and a blue bed for the boy along with nightdresses for each child. Note the box photo which shows the Steffie-face Heart Family Mom and a blond Dad who uses the 1983-dated Crystal Ken head mold instead of the 1978 SuperStar Ken head mold usually used for the Heart Family Dad. $25.00.

1993 *The Heart Family Playground Friends* include three girls and two boys. With the exception of Kenny and Windy, the other three Playground Friends have names unique to India. $25.00 each.

Kenny, #5394

Nikita, #3207

Sunny, #3209

Susan, #5397

Windy, #3206

Indonesia

1998 Celebrating First Year Anniversary Barbie #11908 commemorates the anniversary of the first year of operation for the Mattel Indonesia factory. The date October 9, 1998, is printed on the box front. Barbie doll uses the Mackie head mold with dark brown hair worn in an updo accented by two golden flowers, and she has brown eyes, red lips, and gold earrings. She wears a white blouse accented by four pairs of tiny gold beads, two metallic gold bands, and gold braid trim at the cuffs, a brown suede skirt with gold trim at the hem, and satiny black pants with gold braid trim at the ankles. The box back states, "The Indonesia archipelago consists of approximately 13,000 islands geographically divided into five major islands. In the island of Sumatra lies the special province of Aceh, which is famous for its embroidered and artistic ornaments, influenced by Islamic civilization. This doll replicates the fashion and culture of Aceh and MJD dedicates this piece of work to the people of Aceh who are known for their bravery and glamour." The box front has the MJD (Mattel Jawa Barat) logo, the earth being circled by the Mattel logo, and the slogan, "WOW! Always, above the Best." $200.00.

2000 Minang Barbie #27577 is a Dolls of Indonesia Special Series. Minang Barbie has the Mackie face with brown eyes. She is packaged with two plates, and Velcro bands on her hands allow her to hold her plates. The box states, "Barbie looks radiant in her Western Sumatera outfit. She is stylish in her Minang hat, dancing plates (tari piring), and comes with a do-it-yourself hat." A booklet on the Minang heritage is also included. $55.00.

2003 A Million Thanks Barbie #005.929 is a special commemorative doll for PT Mattel Indonesia recognizing the achievement of producing one million Barbie dolls a week. Her box back states, "Breaking Through The Barrier…PTMI has achieved a memorable milestone…Producing a million Barbie Dolls a week!!! Through your dedication, hard work, craftsmanship, diverse skills and tremendous team work, and with the support of Marketing, Design and Development, the Mattel Brands Operations team and our suppliers, we have finally reached this milestone never before achieved by PT Mattel Indonesia. Thanks a million for all your help to make this a reality!" Barbie has auburn hair pulled back and worn in ringlet curls, pale skin, green eyes, and red lips. She wears a cream blouse with a brown floral-print skirt, blush wrap, a choker, and white open-toe heels. $225.00.

Vintage 1964 – 1980

1964 Skipper #s950 has pink skin, dark brown eyes that glance to her left, rounded eyebrows, and straight brown hair with bangs worn with a brass headband. She wears the same red and white nautical swimsuit with red flats as the American version. $350.00.

1966 Barbie with "Lifelike" Bendable Legs #b1070 has been found in Japan with the rarest variation: a pink skin tone. She wears the same one-piece swimsuit as the American doll, a multicolored vertically striped tank top with attached turquoise shorts and open-toe turquoise heels. $1,200.00.

1966 Barbie with "Lifelike" Bendable Legs #b1070 is even rarer with pink skin and the side-part hairstyle held in place with a Mattel thread and accented with a turquoise headband. $1,800.00 each.

Pale blonde.

Ash blonde.

1966 Francie #fr2205 has black eyes with blue pupils and rooted eyelashes. Francie was sold as a dressed box doll in Japan, and her kimono is among her most desirable Japanese exclusive fashions. A unique Francie pedestal stand is included. $1,800.00.

1966 New Midge #m860 has molded brown hair and brown eyes that glance to her left. A blue headband accents her painted hair, and a brunette flip wig creates a sophisticated look for Midge. She wears a yellow swimsuit top with orange shorts and white open-toe heels; this is the same costume used for the American 1963 redhead Midge. She is packaged with a Midge pedastal stand. $3,200.00.

1966 New Midge is shown here as a dressed box doll wearing her wig and fashion #M1614 from the New Midge Japanese booklet. $3,800.00.

1967 Twist 'N Turn Barbie #20021690 was sold in Japan as a dressed box doll inside a red box with white box liner and unique Japanese Barbie booklet. The doll shown here wears the Studio Tour fashion. $1,200.00.

1969 Living Barbie uses the Twist 'N Turn Barbie head mold with rooted eyelashes, side-glancing eyes, and straight hair worn with bangs. She wears a hot pink leotard and debuts a new body that features great poseability — a swivel neck knob, jointed hands, swinging arms with bendable elbows, a swivel waist, swing-out legs, bendable knees, and bendable ankles allow her to move more freely than ever. $875.00.

1969 Living Eli is Barbie doll's first unique Japanese friend. Eli debuts a new large head with brown hair worn in pigtails tied with blue hairbows and bangs. She has brown eyes that glance to her left and rooted eyelashes. She wears a red leotard that is a color variation of the Japanese Living Barbie doll's pink leotard. She has the poseable Living Barbie body that features bendable arms, jointed wrists, a swivel waist, and bendable knees. $2,000.00.

1973 Tuli-chan #521-26035 has a large head featuring black eyes with blue crescents, titian Quick Curl hair parted on her left and worn with two singlet curls. She has the Francie body and wears an ankle-length pink satin dress with lace trim and a white center panel decorated with yellow fabric tulips. A gold chain necklace holds a yellow plastic tulip. A brush, comb, styling wand, barrettes, and hair ribbons are included. $275.00.

1974 Tuli-chan #521-35033 is a standard version of Tuli Chan Francie with straight, non-bending legs, black/blue eyes, and the original Francie arm molds. She has silky soft side-parted red hair instead of the stiff Quick Curl hair, and her card is pink, not yellow as used for the bendable-legs Quick Curl version. She wears a lovely red satin dress adorned with yellow tulips, and a red tulip necklace hangs on a golden chain around her neck. Red shoes complete her ensemble. Her card front, translated into English, states, "Mattel's Tulip-chan–born from a tulip," and her card back reads, "I am Tuli-chan. I was born from a tulip. I am giving you a pretty tulip pendant. I have lots of pretty dresses. Let's be friends. The pendant is a token of our friendship. The pendant from Tuli is perfect to wear on your wrist. This is a secret shared only by you and Tuli-chan. Tuli-chan's dresses are all stylish! In addition to Tuli-chan's original dress, there are many other fashions. Collect them all!" $320.00.

1974 Tuli-chan Fashion #522-35036 is a carded version of the standard Tuli-Chan doll's original red satin tulip dress with necklace and red shoes. $75.00.

1974 Tuli-chan Fashion #522-31061 is one of Tuli-Chan's separately carded fashions. While most Tuli-Chan fashions are re-packaged Francie fashions sold in the U.S., several fashions unique to Japan were released; the Japanese exclusive fashions that include the Tuli-Chan gold chain necklace with plastic tulip charm are especially desirable. $65.00.

1974 Cho-cho Chan (Butterfly Skipper) #521-16038 includes blonde, brunette, or redhead dolls with Quick Curl hair wearing a satin dress with butterfly applique, shiny waistband and cuffs, and cardboard butterfly wings. A brush, comb, curler, two white barrettes, and shoes are included. $220.00 each.

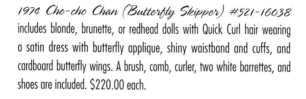

1974 Cho-cho Chan Fashions. $55.00 each.

#522-79975

#522-79999

1976 Skip-Chan features anime illustrations on her box. Skip-Chan uses the original 1964 Skipper head and body molds with dark pink skin and blonde hair with bangs. She wears one of four unique Japanese fashions with flats. $300.00 each.

#S1202

#S1302

#S1301

1976 SuperStar Barbie dolls sold in Japan use a unique illustration of SuperStar Barbie doll's profile with pink, blue, and purple flowers inside a yellow circle, and the large "Barbie" name is printed in Japanese characters. These SuperStar Barbie dolls are actually dressed box dolls since each doll wears costumes sold separately as carded or boxed fashions in the U.S. The basic SuperStar Barbie has sun-streaked blonde hair parted on her left and held in place with a factory sewn thread, blue eyes, and rhinestone earrings and a handring. A Japanese booklet, ankle-strap shoes, and a SuperStar posing stand are included with each doll. $400.00 each.

#A2401

#A2201

#A2404

#A2402

#A2406

1976 Superstar Barbie #a2001 debuts a unique box style that features Barbie doll's illustration drawn in the anime style. The box side and back features full-length anime illustrations of SuperStar Barbie, foreshadowing how Barbie doll herself would appear in Japan within a few years. $525.00.

1976 Superstar Barbie Fashion #b1001 packages the original hot pink satin gown, sparkly boa, and ankle-strap shoes worn by SuperStar Barbie doll as a separate boxed fashion. $75.00.

1978 Superstar Barbie & Scooter #3500 packages SuperStar Barbie wearing a brown suede-like skirt with matching lace-up vest, an ivory blouse, white boots, and a plastic yellow helmet with her StarCycle motor scooter. The scooter with helmet was sold separately in the U.S., and Barbie doll wears the Sears exclusive Marie Osmond TV Fashions #2074 sold in the U.S. in 1977. $300.00.

1978 Pretty Changes Barbie #b2480 is similar to the American Pretty Changes Barbie, but the Japanese doll's box and box liner feature charming anime illustrations of Barbie modeling her hats and her blonde and brunette wigs. This Japanese Pretty Changes Barbie has a much prettier face and skin tone than the ruddy-complexioned American doll. $95.00.

Introduced in 1981, Takara's Barbie doll was totally different from all of the earlier Barbie dolls sold in Japan. The box packaging for the final version of the Japanese SuperStar Barbie and the Japanese Pretty Changes Barbie featured anime interpretations of Barbie, but Takara finally brought the anime style to Barbie doll herself. The Takara Barbie has a large head with child-like features, including a small nose and very large eyes. She is shorter and more petite than her American counterpart, and her arms and legs bend easily. Takara's Barbie is typically blonde with straight hair and bangs, and she usually has brown eyes.

1981 Barbie Your Friend Came From America introduces Barbie doll to Japanese children by featuring the Takara Barbie doll's photo on the box front and including a doll-size poster of Barbie on the box liner. Note the Takara robot head logo that appears on the Barbie doll box fronts of the 1981 dolls and some of the 1982 dolls. $80.00 each.

#127111-8

#127112-0

#127113-1

#127114-0

#127115-5

#127116-7

#127119-2

#127118-0

Barbie 193

1981 Birthday Barbie wears a festive gown with a sheer overskirt and a floral decoration. $72.00 each.

#127153-2

#127106-4

1981 Cheer Girl Barbie is a cheerleader with a striped shirt, skirt, and headband. Pom-pons, a tambourine, and sneakers are included. The box back features an anime illustration of Barbie cheering. $85.00 each.

#127152-0

#127105-2

1981 Wedding Barbie #127107-6 wears a traditional white wedding gown with high collar, lacy white overskirt, and lace-trimmed veil. A pearl necklace, floral bouquet, and white shoes are included. $100.00.

1981 Wedding Barbie #127346-2 is dressed in a modern short wedding fashion featuring a tiered knee-length skirt with pink satin accents, a pink floral headband with a pink veil, and silver heart earrings. A pearl necklace, a floral bouquet, and shoes are included. The box back features an anime Wedding Barbie illustration. $90.00.

1982 Barbie Fashion Doll Your Friend Came From America appeared in a modified box in 1982. Barbie doll's photo was removed from all box fronts. The box windows were no longer glued to the boxes but instead slipped in and out of the boxes over the box liner like a sleeve. $75.00 each.

#127128-3

#127144-1

#127134-9

#127340-1

1982 Barbie Fashion Doll From U.S.A. proclaims, "BARBIE'S NEW" on the box window sticker. This introductory Barbie doll wears a simple dress with matching heart-shape earrings and comes with a free *Barbie* magazine. $100.00 each.

#127342-5

#127303-6

1982 Barbie Fashion Doll From U.S.A. highlights Barbie doll's attributes on the doll's box liner, "BARBIE IS A FASHIONABLE AMERICAN GAL. BIG EYES AND LONG SHINING HAIR ARE HER CHARM POINTS. STYLISH BARBIE IS THE TEENS' FASHION LEADER." The Barbie dolls in this collection wear a variety of fashions that include ensembles for nearly every occasion. $80.00 each.

#127309-7

#127307-3

#127315-2

#127319-0

#127316-4

#127320-6

#127333-4

#127334-6

#127718-2

#127335-8

#127722-4

#633202-0

#127720-0

#633208-0

#633211-0

#633224-9

#633218-3

#633230-4

#127126-0

1981 City Color Barbie wears a trendy ensemble that celebrates a particular color. $70.00 each.

#127123-4

#127125-8

#127124-6

1982 Dream Barbie Collection features Barbie doll wearing her most glamorous and accessorized fashions. This broad collection even includes a kimono, a wedding dress, and an old-fashioned prairie gown. $85.00 each.

#127146-5

#127147-7

#127148-9

#127150-7

#127151-9

#127164-7

#127374-7

#127183-0

#127375-9

#127376-0

#127378-4

#127381-4

#127752-2

#127388-7

#127754-6

#127755-8

#127757-1

#127863-5

#127859-3

#633501-9

1982 Ellie #630011-0 is introduced as "Barbie's new friend from New York." Ellie has pale blonde side-parted short hair and blue eyes. She wears a white cowl-neck dress with black polka dots, a black belt, black pantyhose, and pearl-drop earrings. A black clutch purse and black shoes complete her classy ensemble, and a brush, comb, and styling wand allow her to keep her early-1980s hairstyle. $120.00.

#127602-5

1982 *Flora,* introduced as "BARBIE'S FRIEND," has green eyes and knee-length strawberry blonde hair with bangs to distinguish her from Ellie. Flora is not quite as fashion forward as Ellie and typically is found wearing more basic, casual ensembles since hair styling is a major play feature with Flora. $100.00 each.

#127603-7

#127619-0

#603202-6

#127623-2

1982 Sun Shower Barbie is unique among Takara Barbie dolls since she has darker, suntanned skin to complement her swimwear ensembles. Her box liner states, "It's for splendid summer girls. SUN SHOWER From the West Coast." $100.00 each.

#127361-9

#127363-2

#127357-7

1983 Crystal Barbie wears a shimmering iridescent fashion, dazzling earrings, and a hair decoration. $90.00 each.

#127771-6

#127776-5

1983 Romantic Barbie wears exceptional quality turn-of-the-century gowns adorned with many embellishments such as satin and lace and complemented by a quaint matching hat. $150.00 each.

127734-0

127734-0

1983 Sweet Pop Barbie #127761-3 celebrates the 1950s wearing a retro 1950s red and white gingham dress with a white collar and a red belt. She has a retro ponytail hairstyle with curly bangs. $70.00.

1984 Boy Friend Ken was introduced by Takara in 1984 as "BARBIE'S BOY FRIEND." Similar to Mattel's strategy to wait until 1961 to introduce a boyfriend for Barbie after first establishing Barbie doll's identity in 1959 and 1960, Takara allowed their Japanese Barbie to become a success before bringing a male doll into her world. Takara's Ken has rooted brown hair and large brown eyes, and his body is proportionate to a typical high school male. His arms bend easily at the elbows, and his legs bend easily at the knees. Takara packaged Ken in an easily identifiable blue box that revealed, "KEN IS A LIVELY HIGH SCHOOL BOY OF EIGHTEEN. HE IS A CAPTAIN OF A BASKETBALL TEAM." A small poster on the box liner further entrenched this new Ken into Barbie doll's world by identifying the pair as "CAMPUS IDOLS." Takara Ken wears fashions that range from sporty to dressy to casual, reflecting his life as a trendsetter, an athlete, and the most popular boy in school. $85.00 each.

#1169195

#85-105

#630313-4

#630314-6

1984 Casual City Girl Barbie #290-3 has short bobbed hair and wears plaid pants with a white shirt and red necktie. $100.00.

1984 Casual City Girl Barbie #635201-7 wears a pleated red satin skirt and a red sweater with red and white bow and flower accents. A tan hat and red shoes complete her ensemble. $70.00.

1984 Kimono Barbie Collection features Barbie doll wearing exquisite Japanese traditional style kimonos with obis and matching purses. This series is the most popular among collectors since the kimono is symbolic of Japanese beauty. Mattel U.S. gave Barbie conventioneers attending the 1985 national Barbie doll convention in Michigan a Takara Kimono Barbie, leading many Americans to begin their collections of these fantastic dolls. $150.00 each.

#634305-3

#634307-7

#634307-7

1984 Mink Barbie is the most expensive Barbie released by Takara. She wears a simple black dress with black pantyhose and black shoes with a magnificent real mink coat. A dazzling necklace and pearl-drop earrings complement her high-fashion ensemble. Takara included a display case with Mink Barbie. $775.00.

1985 Candy Pop Barbie wears blue and white striped overalls with a red shirt and a yellow bowtie. A green hat is included. $55.00.

1985 Excelina Barbie #633915-3 is from Takara's High Grade New Barbie Dress Collection. The Excelina Barbie dolls are exceptional with a porcelain-look vinyl and blue eyes, and the clothing quality is comparable to the best Barbie fashions of the 1960s. Barbie has short hair that just touches her shoulders, and she wears a classic school girl ensemble consisting of a pleated skirt, a white shirt with a red necktie, a navy blazer with a metal school pin that has the word "VICTORY" inside a shield, a navy hat with red pom, white socks, and navy shoes. $200.00.

1985 Excelina Barbie wears an iridescent pink dress with a white wrap featuring a diamond accent, a shimmering overskirt, and white ankle strap heels. $200.00.

1985 Fruits Kiss Barbie wears bright fruit and flower-print fashions in primary colors, and each doll wears a head band and comes with a colorful plastic hat. These dolls introduce jelly sandals, and each comes with a bright jelly bracelet and fun fruit-themed accessories. $65.00 each.

#290-2

#290-1

#290-2

#290-3

1985 Kansai Barbie Wao! #635102-5 features the talents of Japanese designer Kansai. The hinged box proclaims, "PRESENTING TOMORROW'S DESIGNS TODAY" and "CREATING A CULTURE FOR EVERYDAY LIFE." Kansai's designs for Barbie emphasize mixing and matching styles; the box front states, "WE GOT IT ALL FOR YOU! YOU CAN COORDINATE VARIETY AS YOU LIKE." Barbie wears a coral skirt with an orange and pink ribbed waistband, a black and white striped sleeveless top, and an orange necktie. Her extra fashion pieces include a black denim jacket, a black leather-look motorcycle cap, yellow socks, and red hi-top sneakers. $175.00.

1985 Kansai Fashions sold separately have clear plastic packages featuring the designer Kansai name in large letters with the slogan, "PRESENTING TOMORROW'S DESIGNS TODAY." The packaging states, "You can grow your fashion image with these dressing kits. These series include Hat, Hair Ribbon, Shoes, Jacket, Combination Jacket, Parka, Stadium Jumper, T-Shirt, Sweater, Skirt, One Piece, Pants and etc."

#635108-6. $40.00.

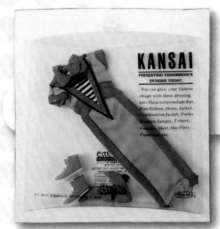

#635108-6. $40.00.

#635107-4. $30.00.

1985 Lycéenne Flora honors Flora's French heritage, and her box front is printed partially with French writing explaining Flora's relationship to Barbie. $135.00 each.

1985 Party Collection Dream Barbie #633506-8 is dressed for an elegant formal party in a sheer pale pink dress with ruffles and overskirt, long gloves, and a satin pillbox hat. A clutch purse and shoes are included. $125.00.

1985 Sweet Country Barbie #633011-3 wears a charming floral-print yellow skirt with white lace trim, a white floral-print bodice, a white sweater, white socks, and large pearl-drop earrings on an outing to the countryside. A hat and shoes complete her look. $85.00.

1985 Twinkle Night Barbie is the first Japanese Barbie to celebrate Christmas, preceding the American Happy Holidays Barbie by three years. Each Twinkle Night Barbie doll wears a festive holiday costume with the words "Twinkle Night" or holiday symbols such as bells appearing on her costumes, metallic star-shaped earrings, and sparkly shoes. The box back states, "HOLY STARLIGHT — Sing, choirs of angels, Glory to God in the highest." $100.00 each.

#635251-0

#635251

#635251

#635251

#634101-9

1985 Wedding Barbie features Barbie doll once again in the perennial favorite role of young bride wearing traditional wedding gowns with veils. $75.00 each.

#634101-9

1985 Barbie Dress Collection Fashions are shown here as a sampling of the many boxed Takara Barbie doll fashions sold separately featuring fashions for a variety of occasions. $35.00 each.

#643043

#643061

1985 Studio L.A. is "Barbie's most favorite boutique in Los Angeles. Studio L.A. deals in the latest fashion of the world," according to the box. Only the shelving unit with base and wardrobe rack is included. $75.00.

1986 Party Collection Dream Barbie #635102-5 is among the very last Barbie dolls produced by Takara, as the company prepared to produce Jenny doll in early 1986. She has light brown hair and large blue eyes and wears a fantastic quality dress featuring a white satin bodice accented by a pearl and a skirt featuring multiple tiers of white lace. $150.00.

Japan: Takara Hiromichi Nakano 1986

1986 American Doll Barbie was designed by famous Japanese fashion designer Hiromichi Nakano using the original 1959 Barbie head mold with blue eyes and coral lips, and she wears her hair in a ponytail with curly bangs. She has white earrings with rhinestones. She uses the straight-arms, smooth unbending legs body of the My First Barbie doll with coral-painted fingernails. The illustrated box lid pays homage to vintage box lids of early Barbie dolls, but the illustrations capture Nakano's new fashion designs worn by American Doll Barbie. The dolls wearing the red plaid coat and the green plaid coat come with a pink skirt, matching jacket, and belt that offer a second fashion look when worn with the black shell. $595.00 each.

Courtesy of Carol Roth.

Courtesy of Carol Roth.

Courtesy of Carol Roth.

1986 Glamorous U.S. Barbie dolls are Ma-ba's attempt to re-introduce Japanese children and collectors to the SuperStar Barbie doll look that had been absent during Takara's production run in the first half of the decade. Each Glamorous U.S. Barbie uses the SuperStar Barbie head mold with side-parted thick and bouncy "bright blond" hair and "dreaming blue eyes" — a real departure from Takara's anime look of large heads, huge brown eyes, and straight hair with bangs. The Glamorous U.S. Barbie dolls wear the best fashions the U.S. had to offer; four of the fashions are from Oscar de la Renta's American collection, Collector Series IV, V, VII, and VIII, and the fifth is a perennial favorite wedding gown. Only 500 of each doll were produced. The story on their box backs, written in stilted English, reads, "A heroine in a book which I read yesterday was splendid, but today I am a heroine. I'll dress up for the party, to have my hair set, wearing my favorite earring, pretty necklace, cute brooch, handbag presented by my dad for my birthday, fabulous party dress, and lovely scented perfume. Let's put on shoes and open a door and then I'll be a heroine. I'll enjoy to have lovely conversation with my friends about fashion, music, and so on, there are lots of subjects for our conversation. I will be happy if everyone says that this dress suit me. Shall we go to a glamorous party with me." This is Ma-ba's only use of the American-look Barbie doll before producing their own versions of Barbie and Ken dolls in the popular anime style. $150.00 each.

#IV

#V

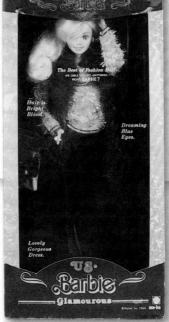

#VII

#VIII

1986 Barbie in New York represents Barbie doll as a tourist visiting New York City. Note the New York City skyline with the World Trade Center towers on her box front. $75.00 each.

#C-55

#C-56

#C-57

#C-59

#P-29

#P-28

1986 Diamond Dream Barbie celebrates the beauty of diamonds in her lovely ballgown, which features a "diamond" cluster pendant, "diamond" drop earrings, and pumps with "diamond" accents. $75.00 each.

#CAM-20

#CAM-21

#CAM-25

#CAM-27

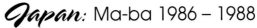

1986 Fantasy Barbie City Barbie Collection #c-21 features Barbie doll wearing a school uniform consisting of a red and black pleated plaid skirt, a white shirt with a red necktie, and a white sweater with navy trim. $75.00.

1986 Fantasy Barbie City Barbie Collection #c-29 wears a red sleeveless top and a white skirt with red polka dots accented by a black bow. $75.00.

1986 Fantasy Barbie City Barbie Collection wears a pink sweater with a red bow on the bodice, a red skirt with white heart print, and knee-high white socks. Pink shoes and white earrings complete her ensemble. $65.00.

1986 Fantasy Barbie City Barbie Collection wears a purple kimono featuring exotic floral print and a red obi. $85.00.

1986 Fantasy Barbie Resort Barbie Collection #r-4 features Barbie doll wearing a hooded pink "BARBIE CLUB" jacket with blue and white striped shorts. $60.00.

#P-13

1986 Fantasy Barbie Princess Barbie Collection spotlights Barbie doll wearing regal gowns fit for a princess. $80.00 each.

#P-24

#P-25

#P-26

#P-33

#P-35

1986 Fantasy Ken has rooted dark blond hair and brown eyes. The Fantasy Ken collection showcases Ken in suits, tuxedos, and active wear. $85.00 each.

#K-3

#K-4

#K-13

#K-16

#K-18

#CAM-2

1986 Flower Barbie Collection features Barbie doll wearing costumes decorated with colorful flowers. Each doll comes with a bouquet of various flowers. $70.00 each.

#CAM-1

#CAM-6

#CAM-5

#CAM-7

1986 Pet on Pet Barbie features Barbie doll wearing animal-print clothing. Each doll comes with an iron-on patch. $60.00 each.

#CAM-9

#CAM-13

#CAM-14

#CAM-11

#CAM-18

#CAM-15

1986 Barbie House #1500353 is a wonderful playset that folds up suitcase style. Barbie doll's furnished Japanese home features a bedroom with a bed, a vanity, and a throw rug; a living room with a sectional sofa with heart pillows, a coffee table, and a shelving unit with a television, a typewriter, a telephone, and a radio/cassette tape player; a bathroom with a bathtub, a toilet, and a sink; a kitchen with a refrigerator, a stove top, an oven, a sink, and a table with two chairs; and a dog's room with a dog. $300.00.

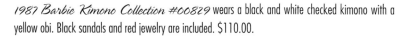

1987 Barbie Kimono Collection #00829 wears a black and white checked kimono with a yellow obi. Black sandals and red jewelry are included. $110.00.

1987 Campus Collection Barbie attends Midorigaoka High School in Japan. The school crest and an illustration of the school appears on the box fronts of each doll in this series. Barbie and Ken meet new Japanese friends Noel and Sophie at Midorigaoka High School, and Stephanie is their teacher. The Campus Collection is among the most desirable of all the Japanese Barbie dolls because of the traditional school girl theme and the introduction of three new characters in Barbie doll's world.

$110.00.

#00845, $100.00.

1987 Campus Collection Ken #k-21 wears a mint green and white checked jacket featuring the Midorigaoka school crest, a dress shirt, and mint green slacks. $110.00.

1987 Campus Collection Noel is Barbie doll's blonde, brown-eyed friend at Midorigaoka High School. Noel has straight waist-length blonde hair and wears several stylish fashions. These are her only appearances in Barbie doll's world. $200.00 each.

#N-1

#N-2

1987 Campus Collection Sophie #s-1 is Barbie doll's brown-haired, green-eyed friend at Midorigaoka High School. She wears a belted pink jumper dress with the school crest on the bodice and a white shirt with a black necktie. $200.00.

1987 Campus Collection Stephanie is the only "adult" character to interact with teenage Barbie and her friends in Japan. Stephanie has titian hair and wears a sophisticated ensemble typical of a high school teacher. She comes with eyeglasses, books, and a purse. $200.00 each.

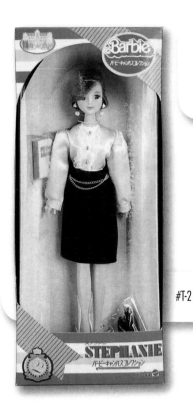

#T-2

#T-1

1987 Campus Collection Barbie High School includes a schoolroom setting with a teacher's desk, four student desks with chairs, and a wipe-off vinyl blackboard; along with a restroom with toilet; a nurse's office with bed, a stocked medicine cabinet, and scales; a buffet-style cafeteria; and a working radio station featuring bells and school sounds. $400.00.

1987 Campus Collection Crepe Shop Barbie #hi-10 is part of the Campus Collection and features the Midorigaoka High School illustration and crest on her box front. Crepe Shop Barbie has short crimped hair and wears a blue and white striped uniform with a white Crepe Shop apron for her after school job. A "BARBIE" schoolbook, lacy white headband, and pink shoes complete her ensemble. $125.00.

1987 Campus Collection Crepe Shop Ken #k-25 has a dark suntan and sandy blonde hair. He wears a blue and white striped shirt with a pink bowtie, pale yellow pants, and a white Crepe Shop apron. He comes with a blue and yellow cap and white sneakers for his after school job at the Crepe Shop. $125.00.

1987 City Barbie Collection Barbie in L.A. #la-1 wears a black sleeveless top featuring a gold chain, a black and white checked miniskirt with white lace trim, and black knee-high socks. $150.00.

1987 City Barbie Collection Barbie in Paris #c-108 features Barbie with a blunt-cut hairstyle wearing a school-girl uniform. A red book bag is included. $150.00.

1987 City Barbie Collection Beautiful Barbie #1500949 wears a magnificent red satin jacket with white polka dots over a black blouse and a black satin skirt. Black thigh-high tights, a black patent vinyl belt with gold buckle, a pearl cameo, pearl-drop earrings, black pumps, and a black hat with a white bow complete her high-fashion look. $165.00.

1987 City Barbie Collection Beautiful Barbie #1500950 is identified as Misty Flash on the box sticker. She wears a sleeveless satin top with a sheer black ruffle at the waist accented by white bows and two gold beads, a black satin skirt, pearl-drop earrings with gold studs, white gloves, and a pearl and gold bead necklace with a large pearl pendant. A large black hat is the perfect accent, and black pumps complete the ensemble. $150.00.

1987 Crystal Queen Barbie is competing in a beauty pageant for the title of Crystal Queen. Each doll in this series wears a magnificent gown with a red sash featuring a golden medallion dated 1959. A bejeweled golden crown, pumps, and a contest poster are included. $100.00 each.

#P-59

#P-60

#P-61

#P-70

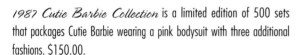

1987 Cutie Barbie #1500677 is the most basic Ma-ba Barbie doll. She has strawberry blonde hair and brown eyes. She wears a simple one-piece bodysuit with white earrings and a handring. $45.00.

1987 Cutie Barbie Collection is a limited edition of 500 sets that packages Cutie Barbie wearing a pink bodysuit with three additional fashions. $150.00.

1987 Hello Barbie is a promotional, introductory-price basic Barbie doll. She wears a simple pale pink dress with a lacy white collar and white earrings. $65.00.

1987 Princess Barbie Collection features Barbie doll wearing fantasy glamour costumes including satin and lace gowns and a magnificent ballerina ensemble. $70.00 each.

#P-45

#P-57

#P-47

1988 Beauty & Dream Barbie is dressed for ballroom dancing. She has crimped hair and wears an elaborate ball gown featuring a jewel on the collar and gold trim. A music box platform is included that allows Barbie doll to "dance" across the floor as the music plays. $100.00 each.

1988 Curl Hair Barbie #9531-383 has hair that holds curls when styled. She wears a pink satin dress with a pink tulle decoration at her waist featuring a pink satin bow; this decoration can also be worn in her hair. Her box states, "Girls can easily change BARBIE's hair to curly hair with curlers. Girls have fun to create BARBIE's hair style variously, thus it can encourage girls' creativity to beauty." A curling wand and hair styling accessories are included. $60.00.

1988 Perfume Pretty Barbie #1500998 is packaged with a .5 fluid ounce bottle of Barbie Fragrance and a large pink hair comb. She wears a pale pink satin dress with a tulle overskirt featuring pink flocked bows, and a large pink satin bow accents her waist and her hair. Her box states, "You can, indeed, go through this splendid fragrance of perfume with BARBIE. Why don't you join now a company of grown-ups with Perfume Pretty BARBIE, though you may be a little too young?" While this Perfume Pretty Barbie doll's dress is unique to Japan, she wears the American Perfume Pretty Barbie doll's gown in the photos on her box. $50.00.

1988 Princess Fantasy Barbie wears a satin gown with metallic gold or silver accents and pearl-drop earrings. The box states, "Princess Fantasy is a very princess-like, gorgeous and noble dress. Princess Fantasy can answer girls' dream girls have looked for." $75.00 each.

#P-80

#4976496

#1500966

1988 Super Dress Barbie wears a change-around gown that can be worn at least six different ways. The dress can be worn long as shown or as a short minidress. The overskirt can be worn as a cape, and the overskirt can be long or short in the front. The bodice ruffle doubles as a short skirt or as a wrap. Her box states, "One dress is changeable to new type dress by combination with other material sets. It is Super Dress. Playing with Super Dress develops girls' creativity." The doll in pink wears an ensemble very similar to that worn by the 1987 American Wal-Mart Pink Jubilee Barbie. $75.00 each.

#1500961

#1501000

Japan: Ma-ba P.B. Store

The P.B. Store in Japan, in a daring venture years ahead of its time, partnered with Ma-ba to sell Barbie dolls utilizing vintage 1959 and 1967 Barbie head molds. The 1959 head mold was the very same as used for the original Barbie doll sold in 1959, while the 1967 head mold was first used on the 1967 Twist 'N Turn Barbie. The P.B. Store Barbie dolls wear re-creations of vintage fashions or unique, contemporary styles. Dolls using the 1959 head mold were offered with either a ponytail or bubble cut hairstyle, while dolls using the 1967 head mold were created with or without rooted eyelashes, with straight or curled bangs, and with straight hair or with a ponytail. The same pale pink box with the signature "Barbie" logo on the front lid was used for all P.B. Store Barbie dolls, and a sticker on the top of the box identified the doll inside, which was simply wrapped in pink tissue paper. A posing stand with a round black plastic base was included with each doll. When these dolls appeared in 1987, collectors rebelled against what was perceived to be a high retail price, but 30 years later the amazing quality of these dolls has finally been appreciated, and it is rare to find any P.B. Store Barbie doll priced less than $300. The original head molds used by Ma-ba were lost after the dolls were discontinued in 1989, so Mattel U.S. had to recast the heads in the mid-1990s when the Nostalgic Barbie and Collector's Request reproduction Barbie dolls debuted, so the Ma-ba P.B. Store dolls are ironically more authentic looking than the reproduction Barbie dolls sold in 2007.

The P.B. Store Barbie dolls on this page wear reproductions or updates of classic vintage fashions and use the 1959 original Barbie head mold with a ponytail with bangs.

1987 Barbie Wedding #p.b.-01db, $400.00.

1987 Black Evening Barbie #p.b.-02br, $375.00.

1987 Gay Parisienne Barbie, $400.00.

The P.B. Store Barbie dolls on this page wear contemporary fashions and use the 1959 head mold with the ponytail hairstyle.

1987 Black Kimono Barbie, $520.00.

1987 French Maid Barbie, $495.00.

1987 Pink Evening Barbie #pb-03br, $375.00.

1987 Uchikake Kimono Barbie #pb-04, $500.00.

The P.B. Store Barbie dolls shown here wear contemporary fashions and use the 1959 head mold with the bubble cut hairstyle.

1987 Red Kimono Barbie, $450.00.

1987 Summer Dress Barbie, $400.00.

1987 White & Pink Dress Barbie, $400.00.

The P.B. Store Barbie dolls shown here use the 1967 Twist 'N Turn Barbie head mold with straight bangs and straight hair, the original 1967 TNT hairstyle. but with no rooted eyelashes. *This only applies to the first two dolls on this page since the third doll has rooted eyelashes.

1987 Black Leather Dress Barbie, $575.00.

1987 Blue Dress Barbie, $495.00.

1987 Fur Coat Barbie #dt-017, $520.00.

The P.B. Store Barbie dolls shown here use the 1967 Twist 'N Turn Barbie head mold with rooted eyelashes and the original 1967 TNT hair style with straight bangs.

1987 Red Gown Barbie. $495.00.

The P.B. Store Barbie dolls shown here use the 1967 Twist 'N Turn Barbie head mold with rooted eyelashes and a ponytail with curly bangs.

1987 Green Gown Barbie, $475.00.

1987 Solo in the Spotlight Barbie, $495.00.

1987 Victorian Barbie #60 B6031, $450.00.

1989 Star Princess Barbie #28533 has violet eyes and straight blonde hair with bangs. She wears a blue satin gown featuring gold stars on the skirt, a bejeweled bodice, and gold jewelry. A gold crown with a blue "jewel," a gold necklace with three blue "jewels," sparkly pumps, and a gold wand on a gold chain necklace are included. This earliest Bandai Barbie features a gold "30th Anniversary" sticker on her box window, commemorating the 30 years since Barbie doll's 1959 debut. Her box introduces this latest Barbie doll to children by stating, "BARBIE's beautiful face attracts many girls. BARBIE has shiny and soft hair. BARBIE is a well-proportioned figure. BARBIE is an ideal lady girls have looked for." Her box back lists a Barbie Profile indicating her age, 17., her birthday, March 9., her blood type, A., her constellation, her native place, her hobby, and her favorite foods. $65.00.

1990 Star Princess Barbie #29821 wears a pink satin skirt with gold stars, a gold lamé bodice with a red "jewel," and sheer pink sleeves. A gold crown, necklace, wand on a chain necklace, and sparkly pumps are included. $55.00.

1990 Afternoon Party Barbie #29806 wears a red and white gingham server's dress with a white blouse, red jewelry, and red shoes. Her pink table service includes two saucers, two cups, two spoons, two forks, a sugar pot with lid, a coffee pot with lid, a tray, and two cloth napkins with napkin rings. Her box back states, "My name is Barbie. My birthday is March 9. I'm 17 years old. My blood type is A. I like strawberry tarts very much. I love flowers." $50.00.

1990 Crystal Party Barbie #29802 wears a tiered iridescent peach ballgown with a lacy bodice accented by a red jewel. She has blonde crimped hair with bangs and a hairbow. She comes with white pumps, a tiara, two necklaces, barrettes, and a hand mirror. $50.00.

1990 Crystal Party Barbie #29803 wears an iridescent blue ball gown with a lacy collar and a blue jewel at the waist. She has blonde curly hair with a hairbow. She comes with blue pumps, a tiara, two necklaces, barrettes, and a hand mirror. $50.00.

1990 Happy Bridal Barbie wears a satin wedding gown featuring a floral lace overskirt and a "diamond" on the bodice. She wears a tulle veil with a satin hairbow, and she comes with pumps, a floral bouquet, a hair comb, a Barbie barrette, and a Barbie heart-shaped locket on a silver chain. Her box states, "Girls must have imaginary world in their daily life. BARBIE can answer girls' dream. BARBIE's beauty is the very dreamy figure girls have looked for." $55.00 each.

#29817

#29816

1990 Happy Bridal Barbie was also sold in varying wedding gown colors and with different accessories. In these sets, a cardboard Barbie diary and a hairbrush replace the Barbie barrette and heart-shaped locket found in the earlier set. $55.00 each.

#29453

#29454

#29455

1990 Melody Dream Barbie wears an elegant ballgown with metallic gold jewelry. A Melody Dream Barbie poster, glittery shoes, and a hair decoration complete her ensemble. When Barbie doll is placed on the dance platform and the music box is wound, she will "dance" to the music as the platform moves. Her box front says, "BARBIE's beautiful face attracts many girls. BARBIE is a well-proportioned figure. BARBIE is an ideal lady girls have looked for." $75.00 each.

#31084

1990 Original Dress Barbie #30355 allows children to customize Barbie doll's gown with fabric paint and stick-on "jewels." Barbie wears a blue satin gown with a blue floral net overskirt, a matching hairbow, white gloves, and blue pumps. $65.00.

1990 Talking Barbie #3980 wears a magenta satin dress with white lace trim and a white satin bow on the bodice, and she has a magenta satin bow in her hair. She comes with white gloves, a gold clutch purse, and pink shoes. Three button cell batteries inside the doll allow her to talk when the buttons in her back are pressed. $95.00.

1990 Talking Horoscope Barbie #31401 has violet eyes and blonde hair worn in a 1950s ponytail with bangs. She wears a pink and white gingham dress with white lace hem, a white jacket featuring two white iridescent-petal flowers, pink floral jewelry, and pink pumps. She comes with two horoscope cards. Her box is mostly in Japanese, but English excerpts of a Jeanette MacDonald and Nelson Eddy biography cover her box. $125.00.

1990 Barbie Kitchen Restaurant #31082 includes Barbie doll wearing a pink and white striped uniform with white lace collar, a pink apron, and a white lace waitress hair band. The kitchen restaurant playset features a plastic floor, a plastic counter, and a backdrop featuring a pair of plastic shelves full of food. $150.00.

1990 Wedding Barbie & Ken #31080 includes brown-haired, brown-eyed Ken wearing a satin tuxedo with a gold bowtie and a lacy white shirt with Barbie doll wearing a white wedding gown featuring a white satin bow trimmed in gold on her bodice and a lacy overskirt. $150.00.

Japan: Newer 1995 – Present

1995 Fashion Date Barbie #62692 uses the Mackie head mold and wears a pink top with an attached yellow skirt with flowers at the waist and white lace leggings. A pink beret is included. The fashion was sold as a separate boxed Fashion Avenue fashion in the U.S. $35.00.

1995 Pretty Hearts Barbie #14473. The Japanese version of Pretty Hearts Barbie uses the Mackie head mold, while the American Pretty Hearts Barbie uses the SuperStar Barbie head mold. $20.00.

1995 Travelin' Sisters Playset #14073 features sisters Barbie, Skipper, Kelly, and Stacie wearing complementary travel fashions. The American version of this set features Barbie doll with the SuperStar Barbie head mold, while in Japan Barbie doll has the closed-mouth Mackie face. $45.00.

1996 Ellesse Barbie #63056 is exclusive to the Goldwin stores of Japan. This collection features the Ellesse Snow Wear Collection for Barbie — mix and match sportswear fashions that are comfortable and chic "with a splash of cheery color." Each doll in the collection comes with pink skis and ski poles, white ski boots, ski pants, and an Ellesse-logo hooded jacket in a variety of colors and style. $70.00 each.

1996 Li'l Friends of Kelly Melon/Meron #16003 is known as Melody in the U.S. $35.00. Courtesy of Laurel Willoughby.

1996 Li'l Friends of Kelly Peggy #16002 is known as Marisa in the U.S. $35.00. Courtesy of Laurel Willoughby.

1996 Li'l Friends of Kelly Shelli/Sherri #16004 is known as Chelsie in the U.S. $35.00. Courtesy of Laurel Willoughby.

1996 Sweet Moments Barbie #17384 uses the smaller-busted Teen Skipper body in Japan. She wears a pink and white gingham jumper dress over a white t-shirt. She has brown eyes and carries a white Scottish terrier dog, a white plastic basket, and a cloth tote. $25.00.

1997 Cool Blue Barbie #23749. The Japanese version of Cool Blue Barbie uses the SuperStar Barbie head mold, while the Cool Blue Barbie sold in the U.S. has the Mackie head mold. She wears blue overalls with a striped shirt and a blue knit hat and comes with a blue Cool Color Streaks tube for making blue highlights in her blonde hair. $35.00.

1997 JAL Barbie #64347 is an edition of 30,000 dolls sold aboard domestic Japanese Air Lines flights. JAL Barbie wears a navy blue stewardess uniform with golden buttons, a white shirt with bowtie, sheer black pantyhose, and a blue hair bow. A suit vest, a map-print apron, a leather-look flight bag, a Japanese passport, and a plastic serving cart with food and beverages are included. $120.00.

1997 Teddy Bear Barbie #18975 has the SuperStar Barbie face with brown eyes and the Teen Skipper body. She wears a pink shirt featuring a white teddy bear inside a heart decal, a white mini skirt with pink hearts and blue and yellow stripes, and a white satin hairbow. She carries a plush white teddy bear wearing a pink scarf. Extra fashion pieces for the bear include pink heart-rim eyeglasses, a yellow shirt, and a blue dress with a pink heart decal. Dressing a plush bear and the heart motif are themes currently used by the popular Build-A-Bear Workshops. $35.00.

1998 Bake Shop Barbie #23960 uses the SuperStar Barbie head mold with brown eyes. She wears a pink and white striped dress with a blue collar, a blue apron with white lace trim, a lace headband, and pink shoes. Her box back features a photo of Barbie working in the Bake Shop with Ken and Kelly as customers. $30.00.

1998 Dress Up Cherry #21638 wears a pink dress with a pink tulle boa, a pearl necklace, and sister Barbie doll's pink pumps. She is packaged with a white vanity with mirror. In Japan, Kelly's friend Kayla is called Cherry. $45.00.

1999 Blushing Bride Barbie #26076 wears the same gown as the 1999 European Blushing Bride Barbie but this Japanese edition uses the Mackie head mold with a short updo hairstyle with bangs. $48.00.

1999 Burberry Blue Label Barbie #24961 is an edition of 10,000 dolls sold exclusively in Japan's Burberry Blue Label stores in December 1999 at an approximate retail of $240.00 U.S. She uses the 1967 Twist 'N Turn Barbie head mold with fair skin, blue eyes, rooted eyelashes, and red lips. She wears a black shell, a plaid skirt, sheer black pantyhose, a red coat, a plaid hat, and black boots. She carries a tote that matches her skirt. $175.00.

1999 Flower Shop Barbie #27159 wears a ribbed pink top with a pink floral-print skirt and a green vinyl apron. A yellow watering can and a white plastic flower basket are included. This doll sold in Japan uses the SuperStar Barbie head mold, while the same doll was sold in the U.S. with the Generation Girl Barbie head mold. $25.00.

1999 Hello Kitty Barbie #24251 uses the SuperStar Barbie head mold with brown eyes. She wears a blue dress featuring Hello Kitty with angel wings amidst clouds, a white sweater, socks, and blue shoes. She carries a Hello Kitty bag and comes with a Hello Kitty pencil, Hello Kitty notes, Hello Kitty stickers, a hand brush, and a hand mirror. $75.00.

1999 Precious Barbie is exclusive to Toys 'R' Us of Japan. Precious Barbie uses the newly introduced Generation Girl Barbie head mold and wears the American My Design fashions. The box style is similar to those used by American My Design Friend of Barbie dolls. The box states, "We combined our expert doll making craftsmanship with sophisticated manufacturing and have delivered her only to Toys 'R' Us stores in Japan." $60.00 each.

#27306, Perfectly Purple.

#27307, Cool and Casual.

1999 Pretty Flowers Barbie #25506 is nearly identical to the American Pretty Flowers Barbie, but this Japanese version uses the SuperStar Barbie head mold, while the American edition has the Generation Girl Barbie head mold. She wears a floral-print purple sundress. $25.00.

1999 School Girl Barbie #23956 wears a traditional Japanese school girl uniform featuring a pleated red plaid skirt, a white shirt with a red bowtie, a black jacket with red trim, white socks, and black shoes. Barbie uses the Mackie head mold with brown eyes and carries a cell phone and a red book bag and comes with a fold-out illustrated booklet featuring Barbie and Reina at school. $55.00.

1999 School Girl Reina #23957 uses the Steffie head mold with brown eyes. She wears the same school uniform as Barbie except that her jacket is navy blue. Note the "Friends forever" phrase covering her box liner, ironic since this is Reina's lone appearance in Barbie doll's world. $65.00.

2000 Easter Treats Barbie #27173 uses the Mackie head mold with brown eyes. She wears a pink floral-print dress with white lace trim, and she carries a milk bottle and a yellow basket holding two rabbits. $30.00.

2000 Barbie Styled by Yuming #25792 is the creation of Japanese singer/songwriter Yumi Matsutoya. Barbie doll wears a pastel two-piece chiffon costume with a cropped chiffon wrap-top, a tapered skirt with three layers of pastel fabrics, a white-print coral chiffon underskirt, and wired strips of chiffon around her arms and head. She carries a lute. $55.00.

2000 Hanae Mori Barbie #24994 wears a fitted pink crepe evening dress with golden trim and a pale pink taffeta stole. Pink butterflies, a Hanae Mori icon, adorn her bodice, along with black crystal beads and satin ribbons, and she also has pink butterflies in her chestnut brown hair. Hanae Mori is a world-famous fashion designer who opened her first studio in Tokyo in 1951. $65.00.

2001 Fruit Style Barbie uses the Generation Girl Barbie head mold. The brunette doll wears a cherry-print dress while the redhead wears a grape-print dress. Each doll carries a cardboard basket of fruit. $25.00 each.

#53856

#53857

2003 City Smart Barbie #B8687 is an edition of only 600 dolls; 400 dolls were sold as Japanese exclusives while 200 were offered to members of the U.S. Official Barbie Collector's Club. This Silkstone City Smart Barbie wears a black shantung sheath dress with short white gloves, pearl-drop earrings, and black shoes. A white hat with black ribbon and a black purse complete her ensemble. $525.00.

2005 A Trace of Lace Barbie #g7212 is a Platinum Label version of the brunette edition of A Trace of Lace Barbie. Her box lid states, "Designed exclusively for the Japanese Collector," and she is limited to only 500 dolls. She wears an elegant black lace and chiffon dress with tiers of ruffles, sheer black hose, and black pumps. $625.00.

2005 Kelly #k4133 wears a rust color jumper dress with silver buttons over a white t-shirt and orange shoes. $20.00.

2005 Kelly #k4134 wears jeans and a yellow shirt with a kitty-face appliqué and white shoes. $20.00.

2005 *Wedding Barbie #j7928* has brown eyes and wears a white satin wedding gown with a flocked-dotted tulle overskirt, a triple-strand pearl necklace, a tulle veil, a white floral bouquet, and white shoes. Four white floral hairclips and a wedding invitation are included. $45.00.

2006 *All That Jazz Brunette Barbie #j8515* is a Platinum Label edition of only 300 brunette dolls created exclusively for Japan. Her box lid features an illustration of Barbie doll with brunette hair wearing the reproduction "All That Jazz" fashion. The Gold Label All That Jazz Barbie is blonde. $250.00.

2006 *Bake Shop Barbie #k6056* wears a bakery uniform featuring a striped shirt with a red bowtie and a "Barbie" badge, a red skirt with a white apron, a white server's hat, and white shoes. She comes with a bag of two bread loaves, a tray of baked goods, and serving tongs. $35.00.

2006 Barbie & Kelly #j7926 includes Barbie with brown eyes and Kelly with blue eyes. Barbie wears a dress similar to the dress worn by the 2006 Teacher Barbie. Barbie and Kelly hold passports and boarding passes that show the pair are traveling from Los Angeles to Japan in March 2006. A suitcase, a backpack, a teddy bear, a bottle, beauty accessories, and a white cherry-print dress for Barbie are included. $50.00.

2006 Made For Each Other Barbie #j9588 is a Platinum Label blonde version of the Gold Label brunette doll. Only 600 dolls were produced and sold exclusively in Japan. Barbie is a replica of the 1969 Twist 'N Turn Barbie with rooted eyelashes and a flip hairstyle with spit-curl bangs. She wears a reproduction of the 1969 Made For Each Other fashion #1881 featuring a ribbed yellow shell, an orange, yellow, and white miniskirt with a matching midi coat lined in faux orange fur, a yellow and orange bead necklace, orange boots, and an orange plush hat. $275.00.

2006 School Week Barbie #k7709 includes Barbie with strawberry blonde hair and brown eyes dressed in a school uniform featuring a pink blouse with school crest and plaid necktie, a matching pleated plaid skirt, white socks, and black shoes. Five mix and match clothing pieces, footwear, a school tote bag with a gold "B" tag, a purse, a cell phone, four hairclips, two books, and hair bands are included. $55.00.

2006 The Stewardess Barbie #j4256 is an edition of 3,900 dolls. This Silkstone Barbie doll's box states, "No mere career girl, this high-flyer turns heads up and down the aisle with incredible style!" She has long middle-parted red hair tied in a side ponytail, and she has blue eyes, red lips, and a beauty mark by her lips. Her uniform includes a snappy blue suit featuring white piping, a matching cap, and a white collar with a red scarf. Blue and white mary janes and dark hose complete her look. She wears golden wings on her uniform, and she has gold hoop earrings, a flight plan, and a ticket. $175.00.

2006 Wardrobe Barbie #k7698 includes Barbie with honey-blonde hair and brown eyes wearing a sheer pastel floral-print dress with tiered skirt and blue shoes. She comes with a wardrobe cart holding two purses, two pairs of shoes, sunglasses, khaki capris, a "Barbie" print skirt, a pink halter top with sheer white sweater, and two shopping bags. $40.00.

2006 Accessories Galore Barbie #G9297 uses the Generation Girl Barbie head with brown eyes. She wears a red skirt with a floral-print ivory top. $30.00.

Korea

1977 *Wonder Woman Barbie* is the first Mattel Wonder Woman doll, an incredibly rare doll produced by Mattel's Korea licensee. She has the 1967 Twist 'N Turn Barbie head mold with black hair and blue eyes. Her packaging features photos of Lynda Carter, who portrayed Wonder Woman on the popular television series. Mego held the license to sell Wonder Woman dolls in the U.S. during the 1970s, so Mattel was only able to market this doll in Korea. Only this one doll in her original package is known to exist today, and she has sold for $2,500.00.

1986 Barbie #dm106, typically blonde in Asian countries, has brunette hair worn with bangs and brown eyes. She wears a silver lamé bodice with a red bow at the collar, a satiny white skirt with white dotted tulle overskirt, a red satin waist band, white triangular earrings, a white headband, and white faux fur wrap. She comes with a red purse, white shoes, and hair styling accessories. $75.00.

1986 Barbie #dm108, once again an atypical brunette with brown eyes, wears a lovely layered pink gown with white bodice featuring a pale pink cloth flower with green satin "petals" and a white faux fur wrap. White pumps and hair accessories are included, along with a small poster of Barbie in a cathedral. $80.00.

1986 Barbie wears a rabbit ears headband, a pale pink satin dress trimmed with white faux fur, and white knee-high socks. Pink shoes, a pearl necklace, and a silver purse are included. $65.00.

1986 Barbie wears a denim skirt with a yellow shirt and pearl-drop earrings. A blue vinyl jacket with red trim and the "B" logo, a blue duffel bag, shoes, and a pearl necklace are included. $75.00.

1986 Heavenly Holidays Barbie #dm103 has blonde hair with bangs and brown eyes. She wears a festive white dress with lace trim on the collar and hem, and a red velvet skirt, a red plaid waistband, a short red cape, and white shoes complete her ensemble. A red velvet purse, a pearl necklace, pearl earrings, and gold leaf earrings are included. $95.00.

1986 Casual Barbie #872-02d wears a pink and blue plaid pleated skirt and a white shirt with yellow sleeves featuring the "B" logo. Pink shoes are included. $55.00.

1986 Casual Barbie #872-10d wears a peach "I love Barbie" hooded jacket with blue and white striped shorts and red shoes. This fashion is very similar to the Ma-ba 1986 Resort Barbie Collection #R-4 costume. $50.00.

1987 Cinderella Barbie #622-2000 is based on the character from popular literature and not on the Walt Disney heroine. She wears a blue princess gown with a metallic crown, drop earrings, and glittery "glass" pumps. A necklace is included for the child. $95.00 each.

1987 Cinderella Barbie #622-7000 was also released wearing a wedding gown with a veil, and a floral bouquet, white shoes, and a gift box for the child are included. $95.00 each.

1987 Designer Barbie has wavy honey blonde bangs and brown eyes. She wears a red satin overskirt with a black "leather" slim skirt underneath, black lace gloves, and a white fur stole. A black cloth purse with red satin bow and black pumps complete her ensemble. $100.00.

1987 Designer Barbie wears a black polka-dot dress with white lace collar, short white lace gloves, and red satin ribbon accents. A red cloth purse on a golden chain, white pumps, and a white hat complete her look. $100.00.

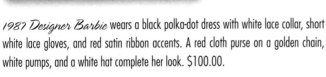

1987 Designer Barbie #622-6000 wears a pink satin dress with sheer white overskirt and white bib collar with lace trim. A pink cloth purse, a pink hat, and pink pumps are included. $100.00.

1987 Designer Barbie uses a different box design featuring snowflakes, but she is shown as part of the Designer series on the box backs of the other Designer Barbie dolls. She wears a slim red knee-length dress with white polka dots and white and black bow accents and a fur stole. A red hat, black pumps, and a pet dog are included. $125.00.

1987 *Danbie #622-6500* is Barbie doll's brown-haired, brown-eyed friend in Korea. Danbie wears a black dress with a white lacy sheer overskirt and vest, a white headband, and white boots. $200.00.

1987 *Danbie #374103d* wears a white blouse with a sheer yellow floral skirt, a white jacket with gold trim, and a yellow hairbow. A pink suitcase and blue shoes are included. $200.00.

1987 *Kotbie #6500* is Barbie doll's blonde, brown-eyed friend from Korea. Kotbie wears a white dotted black skirt with suspenders over a white satin blouse, red socks with silver bows, and a gold heart necklace. She comes with a red beret, blue sunglasses, white shoes, and a red plaid duffle bag. $200.00.

1987 *Fruits Kiss Barbie #c88-730* wears an ivory satin dress with tiered skirt trimmed in green and accented with a fruit belt. Gold lace leggings, cherry earrings, white shoes, and a hat complete her fruit-themed costume. A "Barbie" pineapple barrette is included for the child. $65.00.

1987 Fruits Kiss Barbie wears a green satin dress with tiered skirt panels, cherry-drop earrings, a green net hat, and a plastic fruit belt. A "Barbie" strawberry barrette and shoes are included. $65.00.

1987 Happy Birthday Barbie #622-6000 has crimped honey-blonde hair and wears a black dress with a white jacket and a red and white polka dot scarf. A container of glitter, a birthday card, and red shoes are included. $85.00.

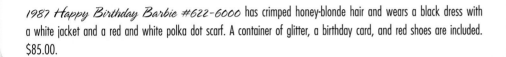

1987 Happy Birthday Barbie #622-6000 has crimped honey-blonde hair and wears a black dress with a white jacket and a red and white polka dot scarf. A container of glitter, a birthday card, and red shoes are included. $85.00.

1987 Happy Birthday Barbie wears a purple lamé top, a black skirt, and black pantyhose. She has a black hairbow and comes with a container of glitter, a birthday card, and black shoes. $85.00.

1987 Snow White Barbie is based on the traditional tale and not the Walt Disney version. Snow White Barbie wears a lovely pink gown with a "diamond" on the bodice and a pink waist bow. A gold crown adorned with "jewels," sparkly pumps, an illustrated storybook, and a tiny dwarf are included. $135.00.

1987 Snow White Barbie wears a light blue gown with sheer light blue overskirt trimmed in white lace, with lacy white trim on the bodice and a blue satin jacket. A gold crown with attached sheer blue veil, a small plastic dwarf, and a storybook are included. $135.00.

1988 Glamour Barbie #b89125 wears a yellow petal-design full skirt with a red bodice, yellow gloves, and a red hairbow with flowers. Real makeup is included for the doll and the child. $85.00.

Malaysia

1994 Malaysian Bride & Groom was created by Mattel Malaysia for the 1994 Barbie Festival. This one-of-a-kind pair marks the first one-of-a-kind Ken doll ever produced for public sale. The Malaysian Bride uses the Teresa head mold. This bridal pair was auctioned for $2,700.00. Collection of Judene Hanson of Dream Dolls Gallery & More.

1998 Kebaya Barbie #23454 wears a green kebaya with a scarf and comes with a purse. Each Kebaya Barbie uses the Teresa head mold, and each doll comes with a purse and shoes. $45.00.

1998 Kebaya Barbie #23454 wears a pink kebaya with a pink scarf. $45.00.

1998 Kebaya Barbie #23454 wears a white kebaya with a white scarf. $65.00.

1999 Kebaya Barbie #24924 is one of two dolls in the Song Ket Series. The Songket dolls use the Teresa head mold with stylish chignon hairstyles. Kebaya Barbie looks elegant in her traditional Malaysian Songket Kebaya. This vibrant blue fashion with metallic gold print and gold woven selendang (scarf) complement her cucuk sanggul (traditional hair pins), gold chain necklace, bracelet, and gold open-toe sandals. $50.00.

1999 Kebaya Barbie #24924 wears a dramatic red Songket Kebaya with metallic gold accents. $50.00.

1989 Party Fun Barbie #6058 is dressed for a retro 1950s party with her short, curly honey-blonde hair with satin ribbon, polka-dot pink blouse, white shorts with pink stripes and floral designs, and pink vinyl belt with silver buckle. White socks and pink pumps complete her look, and she comes with a cardboard guitar, cardboard record and record sleeve, malt, and party invitation. Her box back invites the purchaser to "go hoppin' & jumpin' at the party with Barbie!" $50.00.

1990 Glamour Girl Barbie #8917 wears an elegant four-in-one gown for high fashion looks. Her lacy overskirt can be removed to reveal a short sheath dress or her lacy overskirt can be worn as a flounce or a fancy headdress. A cloth bag, ruffle sleeves, panties, pumps, and jewelry are included. $75.00.

1990 Pretty in Pink Barbie #8898 wears a pale pink dress with a pink satin flower on the bodice and a floral net overskirt and a pink satin hair ribbon. Panties, pumps, and a lacy pink clutch purse complete her ensemble. $65.00.

1991 Dream Girl Barbie #7362 has golden blonde hair and blue eyes. Her box back states, "She's the perfect dream girl in a beautiful and elegant evening gown in metallic gold and lace! Her classy gown transforms into a new style when the overskirt is removed; the shawl becomes a fashion accessory for the lacy skirt." A gold clutch bag, white pumps, white "pearl" jewelry, and a golden hairpiece complete her ensemble. $60.00.

1991 Fashion Play Barbie #8425 has curly golden blonde hair. She wears purple and lavender ribbed pants with a yellow top featuring a floral decal. $45.00.

1991 Fashion Play Barbie #8388 has curly light blonde hair accented with a pink hairbow. She wears a pink dress. $45.00.

1991 Luv' 'N Lacy Barbie #7367 is "fabulous in frills and lace" in her lavender dress with lacy overskirt and matching hairpiece. She carries a cloth handbag. Removing her overskirt reveals a "sexy lavender teddy." $75.00.

1991 Summer Splash Barbie #8902 has golden blonde hair with curly bangs. She wears a one-piece yellow swimsuit with a blue waist sash and a yellow hairbow. $32.00.

1991 Sweet Dreams Barbie #8459 wears white pajamas with lacy pink trim. A matching cloth closet organizer/shoe bag is included for her armoire. $50.00.

1991 Filipina Barbie is a gorgeous collector edition featuring dolls with the SuperStar Barbie head mold wearing fabulous costumes designed by Patis Tesoro using natural Philippines fibers, elaborate beadwork, and amazing attention to details. Each of the 1991 Filipina Barbie dolls is limited to only 500 dolls per design. $175.00 each.

#7355-9898

#7355-9900

#7355-9907

#7355-9902

#7355-9899

#7355-9901

#7355-9903

1993 Filipina Barbie is a second series of exquisite Barbie dolls dressed in costumes reflecting the Philippines' culture. Patis Tesoro designed the costumes for this series, and each doll is an edition of only 1,000 pieces per design. $150.00 each.

#60481-9894

#60481-9895

#60481-9897

#60481-9898

#60481-9900

#60481-9901

#60481-9903

#60481-9902

#60481-9904

#60481-9905

#60481-9906P

#60481-9906W

#60481-9908

1993 Patches and Decals Barbie wears a sparkly jumpsuit with a "Barbie" applique on the bodice, iridescent trim, a net overskirt, and star earrings. Beauty accessories, a "Barbie" decal, white pumps, and a Barbie iron-on patch for the child are included. $35.00 each.

#60648

#60651

1993 Sara Lee Barbie #60403 was created for the Philippines' Sara Lee clothing company. Sara Lee Barbie wears a pink "I <heart> Sara Lee" shirt, pink and white striped shorts, a headband, wristbands, and pink sneakers. $75.00.

1994 Ethnic Barbie Collection. The Ethnic Barbie Collection extravagantly depicts the tribal costumes of the northern and southern inhabitants of the Philippines islands. Plant and bark fibers were uniquely hand woven by the manghahabi/weaver using a back-tension loom to produce quality fabrics. The Ethnic Barbie collection required such extensive research and discriminating material sourcing that conceptualization of these classic ensembles took two years to complete, "bringing to Barbie lovers not only a rare collector's item served with the sole purpose of showcasing these tribal costumes closest to the original historical designs, but also a brief preview of the rich Filipino heritage."

1994 Ethnic B'laan Barbie #61369-9907 wears a costume highlighted by an Albong Takmun, a blouse with mother of pearl platelets in deep black and blue. The somber tonality of B'laan clothing is underscored by their preference for white beads against solid black bodices. The nearly monochromatic B'laan embroidery appears to have an intense interest in rows and field of lozenges, triangles, and chevrons. $100.00.

1994 Ethnic Ga'dang Barbie #61369-9909. The Ga'dang costume is worn with an aken (short wrap-around skirt) held by a bakwat (sash). A beaded baruwasi (long-sleeved blouse), a choker (singat), the beaded attifulan (forehead piece), and the baruway earrings complete the ensemble. $85.00.

1994 Ethnic Ibaloi Barbie #61369-9905. $85.00.

1994 Ethnic Ifugao Barbie #61369-9904. $85.00.

1994 Ethnic Ilongot Barbie #61369-9908. The Ilongot who live in Cagayan and the mountains abreast of the Pacific Ocean wear a badu (female upper garment) and wrap around skirt adorned with finely shaped mother-of-pearl, brass wire, and simple embroidery. $120.00.

1994 Ethnic Mangyan Barbie #61369-9903. $85.00.

1994 Ethnic Tagakaolo Barbie #61369-9906. Tagakaolo natives wear costumes comprised of the bong panayan (embroidered blouse), patadyong of cotton plaid, balyog (beaded necklace), lampad ("necklace protector"), linte ("lightning" bracelet), tungkaling (an assembly of bells, keys, and tikos vine), and anklets. $75.00.

1994 Fleur De Laz Barbie is dressed for "a night out down tinsel town" in an ensemble "exuding an aura of elegance and stylish sophistication." Her long skirt features iridescent netting over tulle and is accented by a fancy rosette. When her skirt is removed, a sparkly mini dress is revealed for a second look, and gold star-shaped earrings and a floral hairpiece complement her costume. $50.00 each.

#60652

#60653

#60654

#60655

1994 Private Collection Barbie #2715 wears a "charming western like outfit with fabulous printed scarf," according to the box description. The Private Collection features "four unique, completely accessorized high-fashion looks. Private Collection features fine quality fabrics and intricate design details that exude an upscale aura and uniqueness." This blonde, blue-eyed doll wears a yellow satin blouse, purple skort, skirt, red jacket trimmed in gold, a scarf, a red hat with gold trim, red cloth boots, a spat, a red cloth purse, golden earrings, a handring, and red pumps. $75.00.

1994 Private Collection Barbie #2717 wears an "elegant gold floral gown." $85.00.

1994 Private Collection Barbie #2716 wears a "beautiful plaid gown." $85.00.

1994 Private Collection Barbie #2714 wears a "Pucci-style cat suit with silver jacket." $80.00.

1995 Beautiful Day Barbie #62161 wears a sparkly purple bodice with a satiny white skirt featuring pink and purple moon and stars designs. A matching hair accessory, a pearl necklace, and white pumps complete her ensemble. $45.00.

1995 Dream Bride Barbie #62147 has cascading blonde hair and blue eyes. She wears a lovely white wedding gown featuring a short sheer overskirt, a white shawl accented with a white rosette, and a veil with headband accented with white flowers. She carries a single white flower bouquet. $75.00.

1995 Dream Bride Barbie #62148 wears a pure white satin wedding gown with ribbons, rosettes and lace accents. Her tulle veil with iridescent band accents her updo hairstyle, and pearl jewelry, sheer white stockings, white pumps, and a single-flower bouquet are finishing touches. $75.00.

1995 Jollibee Barbie is exclusive to the Philippines Jollibee restaurants. Jollibee's mascots are featured on the box front, and the box sides illustrate Jollibee's fare: the Yum-burger, French fries, peach-mango pie, the Jolly Twirl ice cream cone, and Coca-Cola. $50.00 each.

#62123

Barbie 273

#62124

#62125

#62126

1995 *Simply Pretty Barbie* wears a bold solid-color minidress with ruffle trim and a "Barbie" or "B"-logo applique and pumps. $18.00 each.

#62016

#62015

#62016

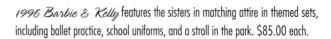

1996 Barbie & Kelly features the sisters in matching attire in themed sets, including ballet practice, school uniforms, and a stroll in the park. $85.00 each.

#15129-9990

#15129-9991

#15129-9992

1996 Color 'N Wash My Hair Barbie #15139 is exclusive to Philippines Avon distributors. She wears a pink and white dress with iridescent ruffle trim. A towel and a bottle of non-permanent pink hair coloring are included for hair-coloring fun. $50.00.

1996 My Very Own Watch Barbie #15131 wears a sparkly purple top with a white print skirt. A real watch is included for the child. $30.00.

Philippines

1996 *Nostalgic Barbie* is called a "Solo in the Spotlight Revival" on the box. Each of the three blonde dolls in this series wears a contemporary version of the classic 1961 fashion, a strapless shimmering black sheath gown with a tulle flounce at the hem accented by a single red rose. $50.00 each.

#62327

#62328

#62329

1996 *Nostalgic Barbie #62327* with red hair is an edition of 300 dolls customized by Richwell Phils for Dan's Dinner Auction, held May 10 – 12, 1996. $60.00.

1996 *Philippine Islands Barbie #15128* is a basic brunette Barbie doll with brown eyes wearing a party dress with pumps. The more elaborate costumes are worth more. $35.00 – 45.00 each.

1996 *Philippine Islands Barbie #15128* is an editon of 300 dolls created with reddish-blonde hair for Dan's Dinner Auction, held May 2 – 4, 1997. $50.00.

1996 *Philippine Islands Barbie Second Edition #15142* is a second series of basic brunette Barbie dolls with brown eyes wearing a variety of party dresses. $35.00 each.

1996 Savoir Faire Barbie introduces "the first NO-SEW Barbie Fashion in The World!" According to the certificate of authenticity, "Barbie doll's gown is made of exquisite trimming, each layer carefully HAND-GLUED, with a bodice that was completed absolutely without sewing it together. Her dress fits her immaculately, her every curve and shape outlined to perfection. Barbie fits in and out of her clothes easily, with a dress tailored just for her. Each gorgeous dress is especially handmade, taking hours and hours to complete. Rest assured that your doll is one unique collection in the whole world. It's totally an art! It's totally a masterpiece! It's totally BARBIE!" Each of the six dolls in the Savoir Faire first edition series is limited to only 1,700 dolls per design. $40.00 each.

#15132-9989

#15132-9988

#15132-9991

#15132-9990

#15132-9993

#15132-9992

1996 Special Edition Barbie #15121 wears the Barbie Fashion Avenue #14363 with several variations. The Special Edition Barbie doll's skirt is green with pink hearts, yellow and purple stars, and white bows, her costume is accented with iridescent flowers, and she has pink pumps. $35.00.

1996 U.S. Barbie #15140 was sold exclusively at the Uniwide Warehouse Club and Uniwide Department Store in the Philippines. $65.00 each.

1997 Classy Barbie #62333-9993 has strawberry blonde hair. She wears a red dress with green, white, and yellow stripes and gold lamé waistband, pearl earrings, and red pumps. $35.00.

1997 Philippine Islands Barbie Third Edition #63819 uses the SuperStar Barbie head mold with brown hair and brown eyes. This collection continues to feature basic Barbie dolls wearing party gowns. The box back describes the native Mangga fruit, the Anahaw leaf, the Sampaguita flower, and the Philippine Eagle. $40.00 each.

1997 Pretty Chums Barbie #63811-9990 wears a one-piece fashion featuring a blue sleeveless tank top with a white flower accent and an attached print skirt with white pumps. $25.00.

1997 Santacruzan Barbie Collection. According to the Filipina Santacruzan Barbie booklet, "In many places in the Philippines, May is a month laden with festivities in honor of the Blessed Virgin Mary. It is during this month when one encounters church processions downtown or on the city streets. Such a parade is called the Santacruzan. A procession of biblical and historical characters is portrayed by local people. For the grand finale, the lady who was selected as Reyna Elena (Queen Helena) walks in the parade under a canopy of May flowers with the image of the Blessed Virgin behind her. The Santacruzan is linked closely to the Spanish colonization of the Philippines in 1521. To deepen the Christianization of the natives, the friars (Spanish priests) used such graphic means for Biblical instruction. The Barbie Santacruzan Collection showcases the multiple participants of such an elaborate procession. Modernity has somewhat eroded the true essence of such a festival. Oftentimes, the parade turns into a pageant of beautiful women. Truly, Barbie aims to introduce a piece of the Philippine's rich culture to the world. But more importantly, Barbie wishes to usher in the awareness, especially to the children the pride they must bear in their Filipino heritage."

1997 Santacruzan Reyna Banderada Barbie #63815-9903 is the Flag Bearer, dressed in a gown of red, white, and blue — the dominant colors of the Philippines flag. Her costume features three stars and the sun; the three stars signify the three main islands of the country and the sun represents the provinces that fought for the country's freedom. She is the rarest doll is the series. $165.00.

1997 Santacruzan Reyna Caridad Barbie #63815-9907 is the Queen of Charity who carries a basket full of coins. She embodies the Filipino virtue of generosity, giving alms to the poor and always valuing the sense of compassion and helpfulness towards others. $90.00.

1997 Santacruzan Reyna De Las Aetas Barbie #63815-9901. According to her booklet, she represents the kinky-haired, dark-complexioned first settlers of the Philippines who still live in the mountains of various places like Zambales. $100.00.

1997 Santacruzan Reyna De Las Flores Barbie #63815-9908. This Queen of May Blossoms is associated with the May pilgrimages. $110.00.

1997 Santacruzan Reyna Elena Barbie #63815-9909. Queen Helena parades under a canopy of May flowers alongside her son, Prince Constantine. Traditionally, the town's loveliest lady plays the role of Reyna Elena (Queen Helena). $110.00.

1997 Santacruzan Reyna Emperiatrix Barbie #63815-9910. Parading in a very regal costume with crown jewels, the Empress is Queen of Rome and is responsible for handing the scepter to Prince Constantine. $100.00.

1997 Santacruzan Reyna Esperanza Barbie #63815-9906. According to her booklet, this Queen of Hope "represents the Filipino's quest for happiness in the present life and eternal salvation in the life ahead. For the Filipinos, religion plays a vital role in attaining these goals. The bird that rests on her fingers also symbolizes the Filipinos' hope for freedom. The Philippines was colonized by different countries for centuries, and like the bird, they wished to soar with their own wings." $85.00.

1997 Santacruzan Reyna Fe Barbie #63815-9905. This Queen of Faith, with the rosary in her hands, represents the strong hold of religion in the lives of Filipinos. $100.00.

1997 Santacruzan Reyna Justicia Barbie #63815-9904. The Queen of Justice holds the scales of justice. Her booklet cites examples of Filipinos proving to its oppressors that "it will always value its freedom, equality, and justice no matter what the cost may be." Only 1,000 dolls were made. $85.00.

1997 Santacruzan Reyna Mora Barbie #63815-9902 is the Muslim Queen, representing the southern islands of Mindanao where the Islam religion is most widespread. She wears a Muslim dress adorned with silk bandanas and a golden hairpiece. $125.00.

#63810-9990

1997 Springtime Barbie welcomes spring wearing a bright spring fashion, which is complemented by a bright print shirt or skirt and pumps. $20.00 each.

#63810-9991

#63810-9992

1998 Flores De Mayo Reyna Banderada Barbie #63820-9992 is the lady in red carrying a miniature Philippine flag. Her costume is patterned after the Philippine flag with the three stars and the sun. Costumes in this series were designed by Nicky Martinez. $150.00.

1998 Flores De Mayo Reyna Caridad Barbie #63820-9988, carrying a basket full of coins, embodies the virtue of giving alms to the poor. $100.00.

1998 Flores De Mayo Reyna De Las Flores Barbie #63820-9986 is closely associated with a popular May festival, the Flores de Mayo, which usually falls on the last Sunday of May. Only 2,050 dolls were produced. $135.00.

1998 Flores De Mayo Reyna Elena Barbie #63820-9984. Parading under a canopy of May flowers, Elena walks alongside Prince Constantine. It has been a tradition for the town's loveliest lady to play this role. $110.00.

1998 Flores De Mayo Reyna Emperiatrix Barbie #63820-9985 parades in a very regal costume, completely adorned with crown jewels, that is truly depictive of her role as the Empress. As the Queen of Rome, she was the one who handed the scepter, a symbol of authority, to Prince Constantine. Under a canopy of flowers and blooms, she ushers in the most awaited Reyna Elena. $80.00.

1998 Flores De Mayo Reyna Esperanza Barbie #63820-9989 represents the Filipino's quest for happiness in the present life and eternal salvation in the life ahead. The bird that rests on her fingers also symbolizes the Filipino's hope for freedom. The Philippines was colonized by different countries, and like the bird, they wished to soar with their own wings, according to her booklet. Only 2,500 dolls were produced. $100.00.

1998 Flores De Mayo Reyna Esther Barbie #63820-9987 is the Jewish Queen of King Ahasuerus of Persia. During the Spanish period, when Christianity was introduced, Biblical characters were part of the Flores de Mayo feast to teach the Filipinos about the Bible. $120.00.

1998 Flores De Mayo Reyna Fe Barbie #63820-9990. With the rosary in her hands, Reyna Fe Barbie represents the strong hold of religion in the lives of Filipinos. $80.00.

1998 Flores De Mayo Reyna Justicia Barbie #63820-9991 carries the scales of justice. $100.00. Courtesy of Manika, Inc.

1998 Flores De Mayo Reyna Mora Barbie #63820-9993. The Philippine archipelago is divided into three main islands — Luzon, Visayas, and Mindanao, where the Islam religion is most widespread. Her Muslim dress, adorned with silk bandanas and a golden hairpiece, truly reflects the Muslim culture. $70.00.

1998 Flower Fun Barbie #63815 wears a green floral-print dress featuring red, yellow, and blue flowers on her bodice and a tiered green skirt with white pumps. $30.00.

1998 *Lacey Splendour Barbie* is a reissue of the Savoir Faire Barbie collection of six dolls boasting the world's first seamless gowns, presented in new boxes, with three new additions in lovely satin ensembles.

#15132-9989. $35.00.

#15132-9988. $35.00.

#15132-9990. $35.00.

#15132-9991A. $55.00.

#15132-9991. $35.00.

#15132-9992. $35.00.

#15132-9992A. $55.00.

#15132-9993. $35.00.

#15132-9993A. $50.00.

1998 Philippine Centennial Barbie First Edition commemorates the Centennial of the Declaration of Philippines Independence. This collection features Filipino costumes of 1898, the year when the Philippines was finally granted independence after nearly four centuries of colonialism. With the declaration of Philippine Independence on June 12, 1898, the Philippines became the first constitutional democracy in Asia. The certificate of authenticity states, "Through Barbie, we hope to 'Rekindle the Filipino Costume' and provide a meaningful commemoration of the centenary of the country as a republic." Costumes in this series were designed by Nicky Martinez. Six dolls comprise the first edition collection. Each of the six dolls in this series is limited to 22,270. $38.00 each.

#63814-9986

#63814-9989

#63814-9983

#63814-9991

#63814-9987

#63814-9990

1998 Philippine Centennial Barbie Second Edition. Costumes in this series were designed by Nicky Martinez. Each of the five dolls in this second edition is limited to 18,500 dolls. $40.00 each.

#63814-9985

#63814-9984

#63814-9988

#63814-9992

#63814-9993

1998 Philippine Centennial Barbie dolls not shown in either the first edition or second edition booklets are limited to 12,230 dolls each. $50.00 each.

#63814-9980

#63814-9981

#63814-9982

#63821-9991

1998 Philippine Centennial Barbie was released in a casual collection of dolls sold in slim boxes minus the metal souvenir pin. $35.00 each.

#63821-9990

#63821-9993

#63821-9992

This Tesoro exclusive wears a Banderada fashion featuring a white blouse with white neckerchief trimmed in gold and an ankle-length skirt of red and blue vertical panels. $100.00. Courtesy of Manika, Inc.

This rare doll wears a Banderada gown in the colors of the Philippines' flag. $100.00.

Philippines

1998 Philippine Islands Ken uses the 1991 Alan head mold with black hair and brown eyes. Eight Philippine Islands Ken dolls model different Barong Tagalog shirts, called the perfect costume for Filipinos since they are worn by men from all walks of life and for all occasions. The box states, "The Barong Tagalog exhibits a certain air of distinction. Historians would say that the flimsy material, the manner of wearing and even the lack of pockets chronicle the lives of Filipino men during the Spanish Era. The Barong Tagalog also manifests the European, Chinese, Indo-Malay, and Hindu influences in our culture. Through the years, the Barong Tagalog has retained most of its original look. Though indiscernible, the Barong's round neck was modified with collars, its straight long sleeves added cuffs and the mid-thigh hemline was skillfully altered with side slits. To seal its national significance, the Barong Tagalog is the official attire of the President of the Philippines." $40.00 each.

#64525-9987

#64525-9989

#64525-9988

#64525-9986

#64525-9991

#64525-9993

#64525-9992

#64525-9990

1999 Barbie & Kelly sets feature Barbie doll with her tiny baby sister Kelly wearing matching fashions. Their box backs state, "WOW! These four stylish mix 'n match fashions help Barbie and Kelly get ready from sunrise to sunset." The fashions feature sleepwear, kitchen attire, dance costumes, and business wear.

#64537, $45.00.

#64537, $100.00.

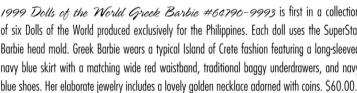

1999 Dolls of the World Greek Barbie #64790-9993 is first in a collection of six Dolls of the World produced exclusively for the Philippines. Each doll uses the SuperStar Barbie head mold. Greek Barbie wears a typical Island of Crete fashion featuring a long-sleeved navy blue skirt with a matching wide red waistband, traditional baggy underdrawers, and navy blue shoes. Her elaborate jewelry includes a lovely golden necklace adorned with coins. $60.00.

1999 Dolls of the World Indian Barbie #64790-9988 wears a magnificent pink and gold sari. A choli in a lighter shade of pink with prints of sparkling golden leaves is worn over the sari. Her hair is worn braided at her right side, and she has a forehead dot. $55.00.

1999 Dolls of the World Italian Barbie #64790-9991 wears a pretty dress in shades of green, cyan, and red. The box says, "Her cinnamon skin tone beautifully offsets her regal accessories which include a copper necklace. From her brown hair to her red shoes, Barbie expresses festivity and magic." Italian Barbie dolls' skin tone is not cinnamon; it is the same tone as the other dolls in this series, and her hair is red, not brown. $65.00.

1999 Dolls of the World Japanese Barbie #64790-9989 wears a traditional pink silk kimono and obi set featuring rich accents of sparkling flowers and leaves in gold. A splendid hair ornament completes her charming ensemble. $60.00.

1999 Dolls of the World Mexican Barbie #64790-9990 wears a white blouse with decorative ruffles around the edges which feature exciting tones of red, yellow, white, and green. Her accessories include two pretty necklace strands with white earrings. A yellow headband and red shoes complete her ensemble. She has blonde hair and blue eyes — unusual features for a doll representing Mexico. $55.00.

1999 Dolls of the World Native American Barbie #64790-9992 wears a powwow buckskin costume decorated with light blue fringe and lined with geometric highlights. A lovely headband in matching colors adorns her braided brown hair. $65.00.

1999 Flower Pretty Barbie declares, "Flower power takes off and shines bright with flower pretty fashions," according to the box. This collection features blonde and brunette Barbie dolls, and all wear floral-print dresses, matching hats, and pumps. $38.00 each.

#64517-9990

#64517-9991

#64517-9992

1999 Sweet Flower Barbie #64516 wears a green, blue, and purple floral print skirt with a blue sleeveless top and a white satin belt with an oval silver metal buckle. $24.00.

1999 Think Pink Barbie #64518-9990 uses the SuperStar Barbie head mold. She wears pink capris and a colorful leaf-print shirt. $25.00.

2000 Angel Barbie is from the Angel Collection of three dolls. Each doll in this collection uses the SuperStar Barbie head mold with violet eyes and light blonde hair. Their angelic gowns are exquisite and are complemented by gold leaf and pearl garlands and golden wings. The costumes were designed by Jun Jun Cambe, and each doll is a limited edition of only 2,000 dolls. $50.00 each.

#64797-9991

#64797-9992

#64797-9993

2000 Beach Fun Ken is dressed for water skiing or sunning on the beach. He uses the 1991 Alan head mold with black hair and brown eyes. $25.00 each.

#48145-9986 Courtesy of Manika, Inc.

2000 Girl Power Barbie is a collection of dolls using the Mackie head mold whose box proclaims, "Hey girls! Good news! Barbie's here and she has the GIRL POWER! Be totally cool! Have fun and aspire to be anything you want yourself to be!" The dolls wear simple summer costumes featuring sleeveless tops, miniskirts, or shorts with satin belts and golden buckles, and pumps. $22.00 each.

#48142-9990

#48142-9992

2000 Goldilocks Kelly #48154 was made exclusively for the Goldilocks Bakeshop in the Philippines. She has green eyes and wavy blonde hair tied with a blue satin ribbon, and she wears a yellow and white gingham dress with white sleeves, a blue collar and cuffs, and white lace trim. White socks and blue shoes complete her ensemble. Her box back shows Goldilocks Kelly with a stuffed teddy bear and says, "Celebrate your kid's birthday with a Goldilocks cake." $75.00.

2000 Kelly Baby Sister of Barbie is a collection of three blonde Kelly dolls and two brunette Kelly dolls. All have green eyes. The brunette Kelly dolls are especially desirable since Kelly is usually blonde in the U.S.

#64791-9989. $50.00.

#64791-9990. $50.00.

#64791-9991. $70.00.

#64791-9992. $70.00.

#64791-9993. $50.00.

2000 Maria Clara Barbie #48139 uses the Mackie head mold and wears a traditional Maria Clara fashion with "pearl" earrings, and she comes with a fan and pumps. $35.00.

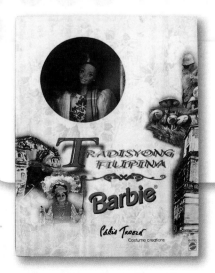

2000 Tradisyong Filipina Collector Series. This limited edition series features fabric patterns and costumes designed by Patis Tesoro. The box identifies Tradisyong Filipina as "the infusion of Philippine traditions into the consciousness of every Filipino... Customs and traditional practices absorbed during childhood and transmitted from generation to generation create a saga tracing the generosity of spirit and love of life of a warm and gentle people." These dolls reflect the unique cultural traditions of Filipino life.

2000 Tradisyong Filipina Anihan Barbie #64793-9993 celebrates Anihan, an occasion where entire communities work together in the fields of the countryside gathering the harvest. A strong feeling of solidarity is evidenced throughout the whole production from planting to pounding and winnowing the rice, stacking the hay, and preparing the rice cakes in celebration of the season. $75.00.

2000 Tradisyong Filipina Kasalan Barbie #64793-9989 identifies the wedding ceremony with the continuity of life since through marriage the next generation is brought forth. In the Philippines courtship will culminate in the practice called "pamanhikan" in which a prospective groom requests permission from the bride's parents to marry their daughter. $120.00. Courtesy of Manika, Inc.

2000 Tradisyong Filipina Paskuhan Barbie #64793-9990 honors the Christmas tradition of Misa de Aguinaldo (a series of nine dawn masses), parols (paper lanterns), carolers, and Noche Buena (family reunions on Christmas Eve). $120.00. Courtesy of Manika, Inc.

2000 Tradisyong Filipina Pistahan Barbie #64793-9992 celebrates Filipino camaraderie and the values of unity and good will through parades with marching bands, processions of devotees, and a feast honoring the town's patron saints. $100.00. Courtesy of Manika, Inc.

2000 Tradisyong Filipina Semana Santa Barbie #64793-9991 honors Holy Week, "a period characterized by displays of intense religious fervor," which may showcase a festive event such as the Moriones. $95.00.

2000 Wedding Barbie uses the Mackie head mold with brown hair, brown eyes, and fair skin. She wears one of four exquisite white wedding gowns and veils with lovely embellishments.

#48140-9990. $45.00.

#48140-9991. $50.00.

#48140-9992. $50.00.

#48140-9993. $45.00.

2001 *Bead Em Barbie #48151-9992* wears a pink dress featuring shiny gold stars, a matching head-band, an elastic bead bracelet, and pink pumps. An elastic bead bracelet is included for the child, and the box urges, "Be CHIC, be TRENDY, be BEADY." $18.00.

2001 *Flora Filipina Barbie Collection* celebrates the flowers found in the Philippines by pre-senting Barbie doll wearing ensembles featuring each variety of the most popular native flowers.

2001 *Bougainvillea Barbie #48152-9990* is a limited edition of 2,000 dolls repre-senting the bright colors of the Bougainvillea, one of the most popular ornamental flowers in the Philippines. Named after French navigator Antoine de Bougainvillea, the Bougainvillea plant is a climbing vine that spreads its flaming colors over walls, roofs, fences and arcs. $45.00.

Gumamela

The Gumamela Barbie characterizes the pretty flower collection of gumamela that comes in different colors. The gumamela is a vigorously growing shrub which blooms with solitary flowers from the tints of white, pink, orange, yellow and red. They grow in single blossom and have no smell. The gumamela is a common garden plant that blooms all year round and with great profusion and with thousands of gay blooms dotting the bushes and hedges of suburban street. The brilliant blossom lasts for a day, closing with the setting of the sun, but each dawn a vast number of new blossom bursting into bloom. Gumamela buds can be crushed and ground up into a medicine to treat people's boils and sore skin.

9988

2001 *Gumamela Barbie #48152-9988* is a limited edition of 2,000 dolls celebrating the gumamela garden plant that blooms all year round with solitary flowers in the tints of white, pink, orange, yellow, and red. The brilliant blossom lasts for a day, closing with the setting of the sun, but each dawn a vast number of new blossoms burst into bloom. $48.00.

2001 *Ilang-Ilang Barbie #48152-9986* is an edition of 2,000 dolls depicting the Ilang-Ilang, a greenish yellow flower native to the Philippines and called the "Flower of Flowers" because it is so fragrant. $45.00.

2001 *Red Rose Barbie #48152-9993* is a limited edition of 3,000 dolls. The Flora Filipina Barbie booklet states, "Red Roses have been for all ages associated with Barbie" and calls them "the favorite flower of poets, composers and lovers." $38.00.

2001 *Rosal Barbie #48152-9991* is an edition of 2,000 dolls. She pays homage to the Rosal, a waxy white blossom with "a fragrance more exotic than any expensive French perfume." The Rosal actually belongs to the coffee family. $35.00.

2001 *Sampaguita Barbie #48152-9985* is an edition of 3,000 dolls symbolizing the purity, simplicity, humility, and strength of the Sampaguita, a fragrant white star-shaped flower considered the national flower of the Philippines. $40.00.

2001 *Santan Barbie #48152-9987* celebrates the brilliant white, yellow, pink, and red ornamental Santan plants which bloom year round. Forty varieties of Santan are found in the Philippines. She is a limited edition of 2,000 dolls. $35.00.

2001 Sunflower Barbie #48152-9992 is an edition of 3,000 dolls. She models the flower with bright yellow rays of petals that resemble the sun. Sunflowers were introduced to the Philippines during the Spanish era. $38.00.

2001 Waling-Waling Barbie #48152-9989 is an edition of 2,000 dolls epitomizing one of the most popular, beautiful, and largest orchids in the Philippines. The pale raspberry outside of the flower complements the crimson inside. $38.00.

2001 Modern Filipina Barbie Collection features Barbie doll as a twenty-first century Filipina woman, blending classic Filipina fashion staples like the Maria Clara with modern styling. Each doll in this series uses the Mackie Neptune Fantasy head mold. $20.00 each.

#48756-9990

#48756-9991

#48756-9992

#48756-9993

2002 Asian Barbie Collection features Barbie doll representing seven Asian countries dressed in the traditional costume of each nation. Each doll in this series uses the Mackie head mold.

China Barbie, #48759-9987. $40.00.

India Barbie, #48759-9988. $35.00.

Japan Barbie, #48759-9992. $55.00.

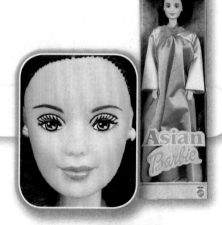

Korea Barbie, #48759-9990. $35.00.

Philippines Barbie, #48759-9993. $40.00.

Thailand Barbie, #48759-9991. $45.00.

Vietnam Barbie, #48759-9989. $35.00.

2002 Cabana Cool Barbie uses the SuperStar Barbie head mold. She wears multicolored striped pool-side fashions with pumps. $20.00 each.

#87003-9990

#87003-9991

2002 Cool and Fun Barbie #87009-9990. This summer collection features Barbie doll wearing sleeveless tops and short skirts, shorts, or capris, each complemented by a pretty floral sailor-style hat and pumps. Barbie uses the Generation Girl Barbie head mold. $18.00 each.

#87009-9990

#87009-9991

#87009-9992

#87009-9993

2002 Burnham Park Barbie #48758-9985 wears a modern Filipina dress with train and panuelo adorned with roses as she visits Burnham Park, known for its man-made lagoon for boating excursions and rose gardens for a romantic walk. $40.00.

2002 Isla Filipina Banawe Rice Terraces Barbie #48758-9993. The Isla Filipina Collection showcases scenic spots in the Philippines. The Philippines is an archipelago composed of 7,107 islands. Blessed with a tropical climate, it is rich in natural resources and claims magnificent breathtaking and historical spots. Barbie wears an Ifugao costume representing the Banawe Rice Terraces, known as the Eighth Wonder of the World; these rice paddies built by the Ifugao ethnic tribe were hand carved into the mountain sides over 2,000 years ago and resembled a stairway to the skies. $55.00.

2002 Chocolate Hills Barbie #48758-9984. In her modern Filipina dress with beaded tapis and rosettes, Barbie represents the Chocolate Hills, a natural wonder consisting of 1,268 haycock hills covered by thin grass which dries and turns brown in the summer, making the area look like oversized chocolate drops. $45.00.

2002 Magellan's Cross Barbie #48758-9989 wears a modern mestiza dress as she visits Magellan's Cross, the site where Portugese explorer Ferdinand Magellan raised a cross in 1521. This is the spot where the first Christian Filipinos, Queen Juana and 800 followers, were baptized. $50.00.

2002 Maria Cristina Falls Barbie #48758-9991 wears a beautiful Muslim costume at Maria Cristina Falls, which at 320 feet high is 100 feet higher than Niagara Falls and the source of 80% of electricity to mainland Mandanao. $55.00.

2002 Mayon Volcano Barbie #48758-9988. Dressed in a beaded modern Balintawak terno, Barbie elegantly represents the world's nearly perfect cone volcano located at the 2,241 meters high Mt. Mayon. $48.00.

2002 Pagsanjan Falls Barbie #48758-9987. Dressed in a beaded jusi terno, Barbie represents the Pagsanjan Falls, only accessible with a two-hour boat ride through a steep 300-foot high narrow gorge. $48.00.

2002 Sto. Nino Basilica #48758-9990 wears a black and red modern Filipina dress accented by gold beads on the bodice and featuring a checked tapis as she visits the church with the oldest relic in the Philippines — the image of the Sto. Nino given to Queen Juana as a baptismal gift in 1521 by Ferdinand Magellan. $40.00.

2002 Taal Volcano Barbie #48758-9992 wears a beaded barong tagalog with a long brown satin skirt as she views Taal Volcano, the lowest and the smallest volcano in the world. $40.00.

2002 Zamboanga Barbie #48758-9986 wears a Spanish-inspired costume with a floral hairpiece in Zamboanga, known for its beautiful flowers and mixture of cultures. $45.00.

2002 Manilena Barbie celebrates the capital city of the Philippines in a series of four dolls that use the SuperStar Barbie head mold. Each doll wears a sheer blouse with a floral collar, an ankle-length skirt, and pumps. The box back features photos of the four dolls at sites around Manila. $25.00 each.

#87015-9990

#87015-9991

#87015-9992

#87015-9993

2002 Ruffles Barbie #87011-9993 uses the Generation Girl Barbie head mold. She wears a jumpsuit featuring multiple print patterns accented by a ruffle on the bodice. $20.00.

2002 Sparkling Barbie. This "simple yet elegant fashionable collection of party outfits" features shimmering short dresses with silver accents and white pumps. Each doll uses the Mackie head mold with different eye colors, hairstyles, and lip colors. $25.00 each.

#87015-9990

#48755-9991

#48755-9992

#48755-9993

2002 Splendor Barbie is the most elegant of all Richwell Phils playline Barbie dolls. Splendor Barbie wears shimmering evening wear with a marabou boa and pearl earrings. Matching pumps are included. Each doll uses the Mackie head mold with a blonde updo hairstyle. $45.00 each.

#87006-9990

#87006-9991

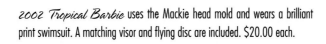

2002 Tropical Barbie uses the Mackie head mold and wears a brilliant print swimsuit. A matching visor and flying disc are included. $20.00 each.

#87001-9990

#87001-9991

#87001-9993

#87001-9992

2002 Wedding Barbie & Kelly pairs bride Barbie wearing a unique wedding gown and a pearl headdress with veil with her tiny green-eyed baby sister Kelly serving as flower girl in one of four different colored dresses. Each Barbie doll in this collection uses the SuperStar Barbie head mold. $50.00 each.

#87004-9990

#87004-9991 Courtesy of Manika, Inc.

#87004-9992

#87004-9993 Courtesy of Manika, Inc.

2003 *Fauna Collection* showcases authentic and rare animals in the Philippines. Each doll is the series uses the Generation Girl Barbie head mold, and all costumes were designed by Nicky Martinez.

Tandang (Rooster) Barbie #87007-9989 models a peach mestiza dress with a printed rooster appliqué on the bodice bordered by beads and using real feathers for its tail. $30.00.

Agila (Eagle) Barbie # 87007-9993 celebrates the Agila, also known as the monkey-eating eagle, the second largest and rarest eagle in the world and found only in the Philippines. Barbie wears a layered, beaded panuelo with a front skirt featuring an eagle print highlighted with gold embroidery. $35.00.

Pawikan (Sea Turtle) Barbie #87007-9991 celebrates the pawikan, a turtle found in tropical seas, wearing a blue and beige skirt creating a sand and sea panorama, with printed sea turtles bordered by black beadwork and wooden beads forming a unique hairpiece. $25.00.

Tamaraw (Buffalo) Barbie #87007-9990 wears a maroon and lavender mestiza gown with a side sash featuring a grazing tamaraw highlighted by silver embroidery. $25.00.

Tandikan (Peacock) Barbie #87007-9992 pays homage to the peacock in her one-sleeved mestiza dress accentuated by a peacock appliqué on the bodice and a printed and beaded side sash as its tail. $35.00.

2003 Kelly Fruit Collection features Barbie doll's little sister Kelly wearing fun, fruit-inspired costumes. $15.00 each.

Cool Bananas Kelly, #87014-9991.

Drippin Strawberries Kelly, #87014-9992.

Lovely Cherries Kelly, #87014-9990.

Sweet Apple Pie Kelly, #87014-9993.

2003 Magical Princess Barbie #87012-9992 represents Rapunzel with her knee-length blonde hair. She uses the Generation Girl Barbie head mold with violet eyes, and she wears a hot pink satin gown with floral net sleeves. A white crown with pink jewels, a dark blonde hair piece with barrette, and pink pumps are included. The barrette with attached hair gives Magical Princess Barbie the appearance of extraordinarily long hair. $35.00.

1992 Singapore Girl is exclusive to Singapore Airlines and was sold on planes during flights. She uses the Oriental Barbie head mold with a black bubble cut hairstyle, dull makeup, and pale pink lips. Her slim brown box is labeled "Genuine Barbie." $65.00.

1994 Singapore Girl Second Edition was widely available. She uses the Oriental Barbie head mold with the same hairstyle but her makeup is vivid and her lips are red. $35.00.

2006 The Teacher Barbie #j4257 is an edition of 5,300 Silkstone dolls exclusive to Singapore. Her box states, "No mere career girl, this professor of style makes learning fun!" She has platinum white middle-parted hair worn in an updo with bangs, blue eyes, and red lips accented by a beauty mark. She wears a white blouse with a red bow tie, a black vest with white buttons, a black and white houndstooth skirt, and black hose. Black maryjanes, "cerebral" round black eyeglasses, an apple, a notebook, pearl earrings, a folder, and a cardboard chalk slate are included. $85.00.

Barbie®

1992 Haute Couture Barbie #60471 wears a metallic blue and gold lamé gown with gold lamé opera gloves. This ensemble is quite similar in design to the American Classique 1992 Benefit Ball Barbie doll's gown. The Haute Couture series was created by Richwell Phils for distribution in Taiwan. The box back calls the four gowns in this series "the ultimate in sophisticated style" and goes on to state, "Barbie carries on the tradition of sophistication, style, and glamour with her lavish gown collection. Whether she's off to the opera or to a charity ball, Barbie is always exciting and full of life, making her a timeless symbol of style." $75.00.

1992 Haute Couture Barbie #60472 wears a slim pink gown with silver bolero jacket, silver waist sash and overskirt, and dazzling silver jewelry. $75.00.

1992 Haute Couture Barbie #60473 wears a metallic blue and gold gown with gold lamé midriff, a blue and gold hat, gold jewelry, and blue pumps. $75.00.

1992 Haute Couture Barbie #60474 wears a slim metallic green and gold gown with a billowing gold lamé coat. The style of this gown is quite similar to Bob Mackie's Platinum Barbie doll's ensemble. $85.00.

1993 Glamour Girl Barbie #61359. This blue-eyed blonde has red lips to match her fiery red fashion ensemble. Barbie wears a sparkly red dress with shiny golden highlights, a matching bolero, and a hairpiece. An extra costume of red and gold featuring a gold lamé waistband with gold bow, a child's red hair ribbon, jewelry, and red pumps are included. $45.00.

1994 Ultra Glamour Barbie wears a minidress with shimmering metallic-print sleeves and a matching hairpiece along with a billowing metallic-print gown with drawstring waistband held by a satin ribbon. This gown doubles as a purse for the child. A doll-size cloth purse, jewelry, and pumps complete her ensemble. She was available in pink (#61175) or blue (#61176) gowns. $40.00 each.

#61175

#61176

1994 White Blossom Barbie wears a white satin ball gown featuring pink, green, and yellow designs, a pearl necklace, and an iridescent white wrap adorned with a single yellow flower. A pink net hat adorned with a yellow flower, a pink purse adorned with a yellow flower, and white pumps are included. $75.00.

Mexico

1974 *Valerie #9331* is Barbie doll's friend in Mexico. Valerie uses the Stacey head mold with a pale skin tone, brown hair with silver streaks parted on her left, and blue eyes with painted eyelashes. This first Valerie doll uses the Free Moving body with a tab in her back that allows her to swing freely at the waist. She wears an ivory dress with orange trim and comes with a matching cloth purse, orange pilgrim-style shoes, a comb, a brush, and a white posing stand. She has been found with both a green box liner and a brown box liner. $350.00 each.

1975 *Peinado Magico 2nd Aniversario Barbie #9332* was made by Mattel's licensee CIPSA. For Barbie doll's second anniversary in Mexico, CIPSA packaged two free additional fashions and a diary with this Quick Curl Barbie, wearing a blue blouse and neck ribbon with a long white floral-print skirt. She uses the Steffie head mold with very heavy facial makeup. A comb, brush, styling wand, satin ribbons, and white pilgrim shoes are included. $250.00.

1975 *Peinado Magico 2nd Aniversario Barbie* #4332 has also been found in a green blouse with a green neck ribbon. $250.00.

1975 *Para Barbie Y Valerie Fashion* #4364 includes an olive coat with brown faux fur collar, an olive skirt, a white blouse with green floral print, and butterscotch boots. $195.00.

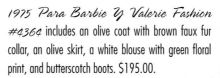

1977 *Valerie Modelo* #4388 uses the Steffie head mold with pink skin and dark brown hair with silver streaks parted on her left. She wears an off-the-shoulder ankle-length green dress that can be adjusted to be worn as a knee-length cocktail dress with criss-cross bodice and collar. White pilgrim shoes are included. $575.00.

1978 *Barbie Hawaiiana* #4390 uses the SuperStar Barbie head mold with tan skin and black hair parted on the left. She wears a brown floral-print bikini with a green grass skirt. She comes with a green lei, a ukulele, and an orange surfboard. $350.00.

1978 Valerie Tahitiana #0392 uses the Steffie head mold with tan skin and dark brown hair with silver streaks parted on her left. Valerie wears a black floral-print bikini and comes with an orange lei, an orange grass skirt, a ukulele, and a yellow surfboard. $495.00.

1980 Roller Barbie #1880 wears the original fashion of the American Roller Skating Barbie, but she also come with the fashions from Jeans Barbie and Jogging Barbie dolls, sold separately in Canada and Europe. $125.00.

1980 Western Barbie #1757 uses the non-winking SuperStar Barbie face and wears the jumpsuit of the American Western Barbie with the addition of a white overskirt. She is packaged with an additional western fashion, sold separately in the U.S. $135.00.

1982 4 Estaciones Barbie #5039 wears a maroon autumn dress featuring a leaf on the bodice. Additional fashions are included for spring, summer, and winter. The four fashions were sold in the U.S. as a Barbie Shopping Spree carded fashion set. $95.00.

1982 Tracy #4103 is nearly identical to her American counterpart, but this Mexican-made version has exceptional facial paint and is much prettier than the Philippines-made Tracy sold in the U.S. Tracy uses the Steffie head mold. $70.00.

American Tracy close-up is shown for comparison to Mexican Tracy.

1982 Todd #4253 wears a purple and gray groom's tuxedo nearly identical to the costume Todd wears in the U.S., but the Mexican Todd uses the 1983 Crystal Ken head mold while the American Todd uses the 1977 SuperStar Ken head mold. $100.00.

American Todd close-up is shown for comparison to Mexican Todd close-up.

1983 Amiga Barbie #5715 wears a green halter top with a white mini skirt featuring green, lavender, and yellow vertical stripes. $50.00.

321

1983 Crystal Barbie #4598 is nearly identical to the American version, but the Mexican doll has a lovelier skin tone and more attractive facial paint screening. $45.00.

1985 5th Aniversario Barbie #6294 uses the SuperStar Barbie head mold with dark violet eyes and tan skin. She wears a red fashion with gold dots and comes with a total of eight outfit pieces to mix and match; this clothing is nearly identical to Barbie Spectacular Fashions #9145, a boxed fashion sold in the U.S. in 1984. $85.00.

1985 Barbie Sensacion #8481 includes Barbie wearing Spectacular Fashions #9143, a mix and match ensemble sold in the U.S. in 1984. $65.00.

1986 Brillantes Secretos Barbie is similar to the American Jewel Secrets Barbie. $55.00.

1987 Barbie Celebracion #9146 includes Barbie wearing a Spectacular Fashions mix and match ensemble sold in the U.S. $75.00.

1987 Playa California Barbie #4439 is similar to the American California/California Dream Barbie, but her complexion and facial paint are much more attractive on the Mexican version. $45.00.

1989 Fiesta Barbie #9585 wears a white leather-look sleeveless top with a colorful tie that matches her pastel skirt with gold glitter accents, a gold lamé waistband, and a sheer pink ruffle. She has very large blue eyes and curly blonde hair. A styling wand and pink pumps are included. The doll and costume are essentially the same as found in the American Flight Time Barbie Gift Set, except the flight uniform is omitted. $85.00.

1998 Mundo Joven Vicky #20969 is identical to the American Generation Girl Tori, but she is called Vicky in Mexico and South America. $35.00.

Barbie®

1998 Hospital De Muñecas Barbie is a repackaged Style Barbie produced for a charity event. $45.00.

2000 Dulces Reflejos Barbie #29344 uses the Generation Girl Barbie head mold with golden blonde hair and blue eyes. She wears a lavender knit dress with open-toe lavender heels. Her box back says, "Put on your dancing shoes and lets go clubbing with Barbie. She's dressed right for a starry night with a little bit of glimmer and lots of lavender." $25.00.

2005 Tu Estilo Barbie #K0417, Tu Estilo Nolee Barbie #K0419, and Tu Estilo Chelsea Barbie wear My Design Scene fashions sold separately in the U.S. $25.00 each.

Argentina

1985 Cocktail Barbie #8909 wears a light blue dress with a shawl. She carries a purse. $65.00.

1985 Rock Star Barbie wears a silver bodice featuring the "Rock Star" label with a metallic blue star, red tights with silver glitter, a red coat, and a white vinyl skirt with belt. Her box back shows her performing with Kenny. $85.00.

1985 Rock Star Kenny wears a red shirt featuring the "Rock Star" logo with a metallic blue star, blue pants, and a silver duster coat. He carries a yellow guitar. Note that in Argentina Ken is called Kenny. $110.00.

1985 Trenzas Barbie #8579 wears a purple dress. Her hair can be twirled and styled. $85.00.

1990 Felices Fiestas Barbie #8890 wears a hot pink gown with iridescent white skirt panels and a faux fur stole with silver fringe. She was released for the Christmas season, so she has an illustration of glass Christmas tree ornaments and green holly leaves on her box front. $145.00.

Brazil

1984 *A Boneca Que É Uma Estrela Barbie* #105140 is "the doll who is a star." She is a beautiful ash blonde bride wearing a white gown with silver and lace accents, a dotted tulle veil with floral headband, a rhinestone necklace, earrings, and handring, and white ankle-strap heels. She comes with hair accessories and, inexplicably, sunglasses. $425.00.

1984 *A Boneca Que É Uma Estrela Barbie* has reddish-brown hair and blue eyes. She wears a Brazilian Carmen Miranda-style costume featuring a white dress with a red collar and a tiered skirt with blue, green, and red satin piping. A red waist wrap, a double-strand gold chain necklace, gold hoop earrings, white ankle-strap shoes, and a magnificent white headdress with red and blue flowers complete her look. A brush, comb, two hair picks, two barrettes, and sunglasses are included. $475.00.

1984 *A Boneca Que É Uma Estrela Barbie* has fiery red side-parted hair. She wears a sheer mint skirt, a matching blouse with sheer sleeves and a lacy white bodice, and ankle-strap pumps. A brush, comb, two hair picks, two barrettes, and sunglasses are included. $425.00.

Barbie®

1985 A Boneca Que É Uma Estrela Barbie #105148 has red middle-parted hair adorned with yellow flowers. She wears a yellow dress with a yellow tulle collar, a yellow tulle skirt, a sheer white overskirt with white satin panels and a shiny gold waistband, and yellow ankle-strap pumps. $400.00.

1985 A Boneca Que É Uma Estrela Barbie #105149 has white middle-parted hair. She wears a sheer turquoise blue gown with a black lace collar and black lace trim on the tiered skirt layers. Black marabou feathers adorn her hair, and ankle-strap shoes complete her ensemble. $415.00.

1985 Bob #105306. For the first few years of production, Estrela called Ken, Bob. Bob uses the 1978 SuperStar Ken head mold. Interestingly, in the U.S. Mattel used this same head mold exclusively for Mr. Heart of the Heart Family beginning in 1985. Bob wears the same tuxedo as worn on the 1983 American Dream Date Ken. $175.00.

1985 Estrela Catalog Page is reprinted here to show the fantastic quality and range of Barbie dolls offered to Brazilian children in 1985.

Barbie®

1986 Em Ritmo De Rock Barbie #105166 has wild, curly purple hair. She wears a black "leather" and black floral lace bodysuit with magenta lamé midriff, long sheer pink, blue, orange, and yellow scarves, and black ankle-strap pumps. Em Ritmo De Rock translates to "Rock Beat." $450.00.

1986 Em Ritmo De Rock Barbie has white hair tied with a pink and yellow tulle head-band. She wears a blue bodysuit with a gold chain belt, a black faux fur stole, and ankle-strap pumps. $250.00.

1986 Em Ritmo De Rock Barbie has white center-parted hair. She wears a black leather-look bodice and miniskirt with fingerless black leather-look gloves, sparkly white tights, black boots, and a shiny gold collar featuring red leaf designs. She holds a silver microphone. $275.00.

1986 Em Ritmo De Rock Bob is bare-chested with an orange flamé-design vest, a black choker, a single black fingerless glove, wrist bands, a black cummerbund with silver dots, black "leather" pants, a chain belt, and shoes. $295.00.

1986 Em Ritmo De Rock Bob wears a black dragon's claw shirt, a black armband, a single silver fingerless glove, a silver lamé cummerbund, a silver chain belt, black "leather" pants, a hat, and shoes. $295.00.

1986 Tudo Que Voce Quer Ser! Barbie has dark red hair. She wears a sheer layered peach gown with a shiny silver bodice and a sheer peach wrap. The Tudo phrase means, "everything that you want to be." $225.00.

1986 Tudo Que Voce Quer Ser! Barbie wears a delicate pale pink and white gown with a pink ruffle collar adorned with white flowers. $200.00.

1986 Tudo Que Voce Quer Ser! Barbie #105159 has curly light brown hair with blonde highlights. She wears a purple lamé bodice with a tiered white dress featuring purple dots, with flowers accenting her waist. $225.00.

1986 Tudo Que Voce Quer Ser! Barbie wears ribbed hot pink pants with a matching hot pink top featuring pale pink sleeves, a pale pink collar, and a yellow "B" logo on the bodice. $175.00.

1986 Tudo Que Voce Quer Ser! Barbie has curly brown hair. She wears a white, pink, and red floral-print skirt, a pink bodice, a white jacket, and a choker with cameo. She carries a "Feliz Aniversario" gift box containing a birthstone ring for the child. Cardboard birthstones for the ring are included. This doll and subsequent Feliz Aniversario Barbie dolls are the Brazilian equivalent of the American Happy Birthday Barbie series of dolls, although the American and Brazilian editions wear completely different costumes. $225.00.

1986 Tudo Que Voce Quer Ser! Barbie wears a pink unitard with a striped headband. $165.00.

1986 Barbie Hair Plus #105256 is similar to the large Barbie Beauty Center styling heads sold in the U.S. since 1972. This set is packaged with a Twirly Curler, a handheld styler that twists and twirls strands of Barbie doll's hair. $75.00.

1987 Barbie E Os Roqueiros Barbie has curly red hair. She wears a green lamé shirt, a metallic silver mini skirt, green and pink chain belts, sparkly tights, and a green and yellow tulle headband. $250.00.

1987 Barbie E Os Roqueiros Barbie has white hair worn with green and pink hair bands. She wears a yellow "ROCKERS" logo t-shirt with black leather-look pants, a gold chain belt, a black fanny pack, and pumps. $225.00.

1987 Barbie E Os Roqueiros Barbie wears a magenta lamé jacket over a sparkly blue bodice, a white leather-look skirt with a gold chain belt, sparkly blue tights, and pumps. A multicolored feather headband accents her curly blonde hair. $225.00.

1987 Barbie E Os Roqueiros Ken #105312 wears a neon yellow "ROCKERS" t-shirt, black and silver striped pants, a black vest with silver studs, a black belt with a silver buckle, and silver fingerless gloves. $175.00.

1987 Feliz Aniversario Barbie #105172 wears a pale pink dress with a pink lapel and a pink waistband. She carries a gift box containing a necklace for the child. $180.00.

1987 Night And Day Barbie #105175 wears a belted brown coat with boots. Under her coat she wears a white blouse with a blue skirt for a daytime look. $135.00.

1987 Noite De Gala Barbie has dark red hair parted on her left. She wears a peach single-shoulder gown with a bodice overlaid in lace and a sheer peach wrap for the "night of the gala." $230.00.

1987 Noite De Gala Barbie wears a sheer teal gown with a layered sheer and dotted teal collar, a sheer teal overskirt, and flower accents at the waist. $200.00.

1987 Noite De Gala Barbie #105180 wears a red single-shoulder bodice with a red skirt and sheer red overskirt trimmed with gold threading. $200.00.

1987 Noite De Gala Barbie wears a slim sapphire gown with poufy short sleeves and a sash with silver trim. $200.00.

1987 Noite De Gala Barbie #105181 has light brown middle-parted hair with blonde streaks. She wears a white wedding gown with a dotted tulle veil accented with a white flower. $225.00.

1987 Sport Barbie #105168 wears a white workout suit with a striped vest. Estrela placed a 12" wooden stick about ⅛" thick inside the doll's box to reinforce her left-side box panel. $145.00.

1987 Sport Ken #105310 wears blue sweat pants, a striped blue shirt with white collar, sneakers, and a yellow hooded jacket featuring the Ken logo. Blue shorts and a "K" logo duffel bag are included. $125.00.

1988 Ciclista Barbie #105104 uses a new body that is only about 9" tall so that she can realistically ride her bicycle. She has flat feet and jointed knees, and her arms are straight and unbending. She wears a blue shirt, blue capri pants with pink stripes, and white shoes. While her face is just as lovely as any Estrela Barbie, she looks awkward and childlike when compared nude to the wonderfully articulated bodies used by most other Estrela Barbie dolls. $150.00.

Ciclista Barbie nude to show body construction and height.

1988 Cor Do Verao Barbie #105002 wears a multicolored striped sweatshirt featuring the word, "RIO," a green leather miniskirt, and yellow-dot pantyhose. A green leather tote bag is included. Cor Do Verao means "summer color." $125.00.

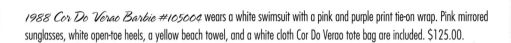

1988 Cor Do Verao Barbie #105004 wears a white swimsuit with a pink and purple print tie-on wrap. Pink mirrored sunglasses, white open-toe heels, a yellow beach towel, and a white cloth Cor Do Verao tote bag are included. $125.00.

1988 Cor Do Verao Barbie #1050001 wears a yellow bikini with a blue and yellow striped vest, blue print capris, and yellow shoes. A yellow tote bag is included. $125.00.

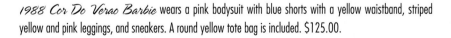

1988 Cor Do Verao Barbie wears a pink bodysuit with blue shorts with a yellow waistband, striped yellow and pink leggings, and sneakers. A round yellow tote bag is included. $125.00.

1988 Feliz Aniversario Barbie #105012 has brown hair with silver streaks and blue-green eyes. She wears a sparkly white dress with silver threading and a white jacket. A gift box containing jewelry for the child is included. $150.00.

1988 Festa Surpresa Barbie #105013 wears a sparkly white minidress with silver threading, a matching waist bow, a blue skirt, and a silver necklace with blue and pink "jewels." The skirt doubles as a handbag for the child. Festa Surpresa means "party surprise." $135.00.

1988 Glamour Barbie #105015 wears a silver lamé bodice with a slim pink skirt, a metallic silver belt, a long sheer pink cape, a silver necklace with pink stones, and a pink boa. The cape doubles as a train for the skirt. $145.00.

1988 Glamour Barbie wears a midnight blue single-shoulder dress with metallic blue threading and a dramatic sheer blue bow accent on the skirt. $160.00.

1988 Glamour Barbie #105019 wears an iridescent yellow bodice with gold metallic collar, a tiered yellow skirt and sheer yellow overskirt, and a yellow boa. $145.00.

1988 Glamour Barbie # 105020 is a blonde bride wearing a pink dotted tulle veil, a sleeveless white wedding gown with white lace overlay, a tiered sheer white dress with white lace trim, a pink waistband, white fingerless gloves, and a spray of flowers on the skirt. $200.00.

1988 Moda Em Dobro Barbie wears a pink dress with green and blue swirl designs, pink earrings, and a silver belt. A green skirt and a green shirt with a sparkly floral appliqué are included for a second look. Moda em dobro means "fashion in double." $130.00.

1988 Glamour Barbie #105017 has platinum blonde hair and green eyes. She wears a mint green gown with overskirt with a shiny golden belt. $175.00.

1988 New Wave Barbie has curly yellow and pale blue hair worn with an orange tulle hair band. She wears gold pants with a green belt, an orange top, and an orange jacket covered with stars. $150.00.

1988 New Wave Barbie #105008 has curly pink and blonde hair. She wears a pink blouse, an iridescent green miniskirt with a green belt, a sleeveless yellow jacket, and pink net leggings. $165.00.

1988 New Wave Ken #105315 wears shiny silver pants, a lime green shirt with silver streaks, and a metallic silver jacket. He carries a metallic fuchsia guitar. $150.00.

1988 New Wave Barbie #105006 has a curly blue and pink hairpiece. She wears a shiny silver shirt featuring yellow star accents, a metallic blue belt, a white miniskirt, and blue and pink leggings. She carries a silver microphone. $150.00.

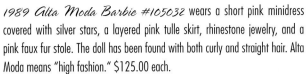

1989 Alta Moda Barbie #105032 wears a short pink minidress covered with silver stars, a layered pink tulle skirt, rhinestone jewelry, and a pink faux fur stole. The doll has been found with both curly and straight hair. Alta Moda means "high fashion." $125.00 each.

1989 Banho De Sol Barbie #105042 has crimped blonde hair with bangs. She wears a one-piece orange and blue swimsuit. Her skin darkens when exposed to direct sunlight to simulate sun tanning. Banho De Sol means "sun bath." $100.00.

1989 Cor Do Verao Barbie #105021 has curly ash blonde hair. She wears an orange swimsuit, a pink jacket featuring yellow dots and yellow stripes, and striped yellow and pink shorts. She carries a striped yellow and pink duffel bag. $110.00.

1989 Cor Do Verao Barbie #105023 wears a one-piece pink swimsuit with colorful print pants. She carries a print tote bag. $110.00.

1989 Cor Do Verao Viky #105400 uses the Steffie face with green eyes, brown hair with silver streaks parted on her left, and freckles. She wears a one-piece swimsuit, a pearl necklace and earrings, a white and blue striped jacket with pink stripes on the collar and waistband, and a matching skirt. Her jacket has been found with both slim and wide blue stripes. She carries a blue tote bag featuring a sailboat. $200.00.

1989 Feliz Aniversario Barbie #105027 wears a pale pink dress with a green jacket featuring metallic pink accents and a metallic pink belt. A cardboard gift box is included for the child. $135.00.

1989 Glamour Barbie #105433 wears a sheer rose-print tiered floral skirt, a matching shawl accented by a single rose, and a pink bodice. $150.00.

1989 Glamour Barbie #105434 wears a dramatic blue gown with a matching blue stole and a silver necklace featuring pink and blue "jewels." $150.00.

1989 Glamour Barbie #105435 wears a fuchsia satin skirt with a lavender jacket with shiny pink and silver trim. $150.00.

1989 Glamour Diva #105422 has platinum blonde hair and green eyes. Diva wears a sophisticated black top dotted with silver accents, a matching hat with black netting, a layered white skirt with black dots, and metallic silver pumps. $195.00.

1989 Glamour Barbie #105036 wears a white bridal gown with a dramatic collar with a lacy border with silver threading, a full skirt with sheer lace-trimmed overskirt, and a net veil accented with white flowers. She carries a bouquet of white flowers. $175.00.

1989 Moda Em Dobro Barbie #105026 wears a pastel floral-print skirt with a plum jacket and a pink scarf. A pink blouse/minidress with a pastel floral-print miniskirt is included for a second look. $110.00.

1989 Moda Em Dobro Lia #105410 uses the Steffie head mold with pale skin, sandy blonde hair, blue eyes, and red lips. She wears a black and white striped sweater with a red collar and red sleeves, an attached red skirt, and a red beret. Black slacks are included. $275.00.

1989 Passeio Barbie #105030 wears a ribbed white blouse, a white floral-print skirt with an aqua blue waist band and an aqua tulle underskirt, and pink jewelry. Passeio means "stroll." $120.00.

1989 Passeio Barbie has brown hair and blue eyes. She wears a red shirt under a belted beige coat with a red collar and a red hat. $155.00.

1989 Passeio Ken #105323 wears khaki pants, a red shirt, and an olive jacket with red cuffs. $100.00.

1989 Passeio Viky #105402 uses the Steffie head mold with curly red hair with green eyes and freckles. She wears a white blouse with lace collar and a full black skirt with white polka dots and a red floral waist accent. Mattel U.S. presented this Passeio Viky doll to each of the 500 convention-eers attending the 1989 national Barbie convention in Garden Grove, California. $150.00.

1989 Rock Star Barbie #105024 leads the band in yellow pedal pushers, a black miniskirt with shiny blue dots, and a blue shirt with yellow sleeves and a musical note/guitar decal. Each doll in the Rock Star series comes with a guitar and a metallic silver microphone, and each of the girls wears star-shaped earrings. $100.00.

1989 Rock Star Diva #105421 uses the Diva head mold with green eyes. Diva has silver ash blonde hair with white streaks tied with a pink tulle hairbow. She wears a mint green bodysuit with a white miniskirt, a metallic pink belt, a white jacket with green collar, and a green necklace. $145.00.

1989 Rock Star Lia #105411 uses the Steffie head mold with light brown hair tied with a blue tulle hairbow and blue eyes. She wears an orange miniskirt with an iridescent blue bodice, an orange jacket, an orange necklace, and orange leggings. $165.00.

1989 Rock Star Viky #105401 uses the Steffie head mold with blonde hair tied with a green tulle hairbow. She has green eyes and freckles. She wears a pink leggings with black dots on the legs, a matching pink top with black dots on the sleeves, and a black leather miniskirt with a metallic pink belt. $165.00.

1989 Sonho De Perfume Barbie #105040 wears a pink ballgown featuring a pink satin bow on the pale pink bodice, a tiered pink tulle dress, a bow-shaped necklace, and a ruffled pink tulle stole. She is packaged with a bottle of Barbie perfume and a hair comb. Sonho de perfume means "perfume dream." $95.00.

1989 Laco De Perfume Lia #105412 uses the Steffie head mold with light brown hair, pale skin, blue eyes, and red lips. She wears a blue gown featuring a blue overskirt with flocked blue bows, a matching attached sheer blue stole, and a pearl necklace. She is packaged with a blue locket containing solid fragrance. $250.00.

1990 Alta Costura Barbie #105058 wears a blue dress featuring blue floral lace overlay and blue lapels, along with a dramatic blue coat. Alta costura means "quality sewing." $165.00.

1990 Alta Costura Barbie #105060 wears a print skirt, a pea-colored jacket, a shiny gold necklace, and a hat. $150.00.

1990 Alta Costura Barbie #105061 wears a gold lamé blouse, a gold chain necklace, a leopard-print skirt, black pantyhose, and a black hat with a gold hatband. $165.00.

1990 Alta Costura Barbie #105063 has short curly blonde hair and green eyes. She wears a short black dress, black pantyhose, and a beige coat with leopard-print cuffs, a matching hat, and a black scarf. $185.00.

1990 Alta Costura Barbie #105064 wears a white blouse with black polka dots, a black miniskirt, a red coat, a black hat with red bow, a black scarf with white dots, and red pumps. $165.00.

1990 Alta Costura Lia #105414 uses the Steffie head mold with sandy blonde hair and blue eyes. She wears a blue paisley and floral-print dress, a blue hat with print hatband, and metallic silver pumps. $240.00.

1990 Amigos Da Selva Viky #105404 is one of the "friends of the jungle" using the Steffie head mold with brown eyes, freckles, red lips, and brown hair. She wears an orange and black leopard-print top with a matching headband, a yellow satin skirt with gold waistband, yellow giraffe earrings, and yellow boots. She carries a lion cub. $275.00.

1989 Animal Loving Nikki #1352 is the American equivalent of Amigos Da Selva Viky, except her costume is purple and pink, and Nikki uses the Oriental Barbie head mold. Nikki also comes with a lion cub. $20.00.

1990 Charme Em Lingerie Barbie #105038 wears a pink nightgown and a matching pink robe with lacy sleeves. $115.00.

1990 Charme Em Lingerie Barbie wears a pink and yellow teddy featuring a yellow bow on the bodice and green earrings. $95.00.

1990 Fim De Semana Barbie #105048 wears a white satin skirt with a blue top, a metallic magenta jacket and matching belt, and magenta pumps. Her purse has a gold chain and matches her jacket. Fim de semana means "weekend." $145.00.

1990 Moda Festa Barbie #105053 wears a pink gown with tiered pink skirts, shiny golden trim, and a pink stole for the "fashion party." $150.00.

1990 Moda Festa Barbie #105056 has green eyes and wears a sleeveless emerald gown with tiered sheer emerald skirt panels, a gold lamé bodice, and an emerald sash. She carries a gold lamé purse. $150.00.

1990 Moda Festa Barbie #105055 wears a lavender bodice with metallic accents, a lavender skirt with sheer overskirt and a lavender sash, a silver necklace with pink and blue "jewels," and a plush lilac faux fur stole. $140.00.

1990 Moda Festa Barbie #105054 wears a slim black dress with black velvet dots, a yellow stole, and a gold necklace with "jewels." $140.00.

1990 Moda Festa Barbie #105057 wears a white satin wedding gown overlaid with white lace featuring a sheer white skirt trimmed with lace. Her tulle veil is accented with white flowers, and she carries a bouquet of white flowers. $165.00.

1991 Baile De Máscaras Barbie #105097 wears a shimmery white minidress with a sheer pink skirt and pink ruffled stole for the "masquerade ball." $95.00.

1991 Esporte Total Viky #105407 has the Steffie face with light brown hair, brown eyes, and freckles. She wears a teal swimsuit with pastel floral-print white pants and a pink hair ribbon. Her cloth carry bag matches her pants. $150.00.

1991 Noite De Sonhos Barbie #105096 wears a white wedding gown featuring a white floral-lace overlay, a white tulle skirt, and a tulle veil. She carries a bouquet of pink and white flowers. Noite de sonhos means "night of dreams." $150.00.

1991 Outono Inverno Barbie #105088 wears a mustard-colored dress with a brown and green camouflage jacket. Outono Inverno means "autumn winter." $125.00.

1991 *Outono Inverno Lia #105416* has the Steffie head mold with light brown hair with blonde streaks, brown eyes, and pink lips. She wears a striped red and orange sweater with metallic threading, a black skirt, and a white hat. $160.00.

1991 *Sonho De Ferias Barbie* wears a sleeveless blue top with a white print skirt. $75.00.

1991 *Tempo De Festas Barbie #105098* wears a "party time" tiered petal blue skirt with glittery petals, an iridescent blue bodice, a glittery blue stole, and metallic silver pumps. $125.00.

1992 *Primavera Verao Skipper #104224* wears a pink party dress with a sparkly bodice and striped white skirt. $95.00.

1992 Festa De Casamento Viky #105408 is the bride of Alan, Ken doll's friend who debuted in 1964; Alan's name was originally spelled Allan but an "l" was dropped when he was reintroduced in the U.S. in 1991. Since Viky is the Brazilian equivalent of the American Midge, Viky married Alan in Brazil. Viky has dark red hair, green eyes, tan skin, and freckles. She wears a white wedding gown with silver threading and a white tulle veil. Her skirt and lacy sleeves can be removed to reveal a white minidress, and a lavender jacket with white lapels is included to create Viky's going-away fashion. She carries a pink floral bouquet. Festa de casamento means "marriage party." $250.00.

1991 Wedding Day Midge #9606 is shown here for contrast to Festa De Casamento Viky. Midge uses the Diva head mold with fair skin and violet eyes. $25.00.

1992 Super Star Barbie #104420 is very similar to the Lights & Lace Barbie sold in the U.S. in 1991 but her costume is a paler pink with some fabric variation, and the Estrela doll has darker tan skin. She wears a pink dress featuring a tiered lacy pink skirt, a lacy pink jacket, a pink tulle hairbow, a flashing pink waist ornament, and pink boots. $100.00.

1992 Super Star Kira #105440 wears a yellow lace costume very similar to the fashion worn by Lights & Lace Christie in the U.S., but Super Star Kira uses the Oriental Barbie head mold. This is the first Asian friend of Barbie doll sold in Brazil. $135.00.

1992 Super Star Lara #105425 uses the Diva head mold with light brown hair with blonde highlights accented by a blue tulle hairbow. She wears a blue dress featuring a tiered lacy blue skirt, a lacy blue jacket, a flashing blue waist ornament, and blue boots. In the U.S. Lights & Lace Teresa wore a fashion very similar to Super Star Lara's. $150.00.

1992 Veterinaria Barbie #104430 wears a pink dress with a ruffle at the hem and a white doctor's coat. A stethoscope is around her neck, and she comes with a plastic dog. The box calls her, "A AMIGA DOS ANIMALS" meaning "a friend of animals." $125.00.

1993 Country Tina uses the Steffie head mold with tan skin, blue eyes with green eyeshadow, black hair, and red lips. Her red, black, and gold western costume is very similar to that worn by the American Western Stampin' Tara Lynn, but Tara Lynn has pale skin and different eye makeup. $150.00.

1993 Festa De Aniversario Barbie #105585 wears a shimmery pale blue bodice and a satiny white skirt decorated with pink and blue ruffles trimmed in gold thread and floral and confetti print designs. She has a white satin hairbow in her hair and carries a plastic birthday cake. She is very similar to the American 1993 Birthday Party Barbie. $55.00.

1993 Fim De Semana Campo Barbie #105613 wears a pink floral sundress with a white hat. She carries a white basket of flowers. $45.00.

1993 Moda Facil Barbie #105510 wears a blue and pink bodysuit with a pink tie-on skirt and pink pumps. Her costume is identical to the American Fashion Play Barbie sold in 1992, but this Brazilian version has a different hairstyle. Moda facil means "easy dress." $30.00.

1994 Star Hair Debora #105621 is nearly identical to the American 1993 Hollywood Hair Teresa, but she is called Debora in Brazil. She has brown eyes and ankle-length sandy blonde hair. Her Star Hair spray causes her hair to turn pink, and the orange plastic stencil allows the child to create pink star shapes in her hair. She wears a gold lamé bodice and skirt, an orange vest decorated with shiny gold stars, a matching orange skirt, and gold star earrings. $150.00.

1995 Criacoes Exclusivas Conrado Segreto Barbie showcases the talents of renowned Brazilian designer Conrado Segreto. His signed original illustrations of the dolls in this series are shown on the box backs. $175.00 each.

#104461 wears a navy blue dress with white satin ribbon accents at the skirt hem and dramatic white lapels, white cuffs, and buttons on the jacket. $175.00.

#104462 wears a slim black velvet dress with flounce and a black net cape tied with a black satin bow. $175.00.

#104464 wears a green, red, and black plaid dress featuring tiered skirt panels and a black and gold bow waist accent. $175.00.

1995 Fala 10,000 Frases! Barbie #14127 is the Brazilian version of the Super Talk Barbie sold worldwide. The Estrela logo is on her box front, and the box is printed in Portugese, the official language of Brazil. $50.00.

1995 Riviera Barbie #105633 has dark tan skin. She wears a pink dress with yellow swirl designs and a yellow ruffle accent. Her costume is very similar to that worn by the American 1995 Ruffle Fun Barbie. $30.00.

1989 Dia De Esporte Mãe E Filha #106004 is the Brazilian Mrs. Heart; in Brazil, The Heart Family is known as the Familia Coracao. As in the U.S., the mother uses the Kelley head mold from the 1980 Starr series. Mom has brown hair with blonde highlights, and she wears a pink sweatshirt with a blue collar and a blue waistband and pink sweatpants. Her toddler daughter wears a pink romper with blue trim, and blue ribbons accent her hair. $150.00.

1989 Dia De Passear Mãe E Filha #106002 includes Mom wearing a turquoise dress with black neckline and tiered skirt featuring black polka dots and a black bow. Her daughter wears a turquoise dress with a pink collar and white tights. Dia de passear means "day to walk." $195.00.

1990 Chegada Do Nene Mãe E Recem-Nascido #106021 is the "New Arrival" mom with dark blonde hair. She wears a lavender blouse, a yellow scarf, a pink skirt, and a belt. She comes with a white floral-print maternity smock and her newborn infant wearing a yellow romper featuring a bunny sticker. $175.00.

1990 Dia De Esporte Mãe E Filha #106007 has light brown hair with silver streaks. She wears a pink, blue, and turquoise striped sweatshirt with turquoise pants and a blue headband. Her daughter wears a blue, pink, and turquoise striped jumpsuit and a pink hairbow. $150.00.

1990 Dia De Festa Pai E Filha #106035 is the Brazilian Heart Family father. This version uses the 1983-dated Crystal Ken head mold, while most Caucasian Heart Family fathers use the SuperStar Ken head mold. He wears a blue suit with a white shirt, a black belt, and a pink necktie. His daughter wears a lavender shirt with a white collar, a lavender floral-print skirt, a party hat, and lacy white leggings. A gift box is included for the girl's birthday present. $150.00.

1985 The Heart Family Dad #9079 from the U.S. has the SuperStar Ken head mold. He is shown for comparision to the Brazilian Dad with the Crystal Ken head mold. $25.00.

1981 Superstar Barbie wears a sheer white and sky blue gown with floral-print over-skirt and matching shawl. She carries a white purse. $200.00.

1983 Muneca Barbie wears a one-piece sparkly purple swimsuit with silver trim. A white satin "Miss Playa" banner is draped across her chest, and a white wrap skirt with silver trim completes her costume. $95.00.

1989 Workout Barbie has strawberry blonde hair and wears a unique black and pink leotard with a pink and black headband. A duffel bag is included. $85.00.

1990 Garden Party Ken #1502572-c wears a white tuxedo with a lavender shirt, cummerbund, and bowtie and white socks and shoes. He is the companion doll to Garden Party Barbie, who was sold in the U.S. although Ken only appeared in Peru. $65.00.

Venezuela

1986 Barbie and the Rockers Barbie #51-0237 was produced by Rotoplast. She has many variations from the American edition, including her black jacket, dull silver bodice, satin miniskirt, dark blonde hair, black hairpiece, and white Rockers t-shirt. Her eye color is blue-gray (almost turquoise), and her eye shadow differs. Her box back shows the American box picture of all five Rockers. $140.00.

The American Rocker Barbie is shown on the left next to the Venezuelan version to show the differences in costume, hair, and makeup.

1986 Tropical Miko #2056 wears a swimsuit similar to that worn by the American Tropical Miko, but the Venezuelan Miko uses the SuperStar Barbie head mold, while the American Miko has the Oriental Barbie head mold! $200.00.

1987 De Moda Barbie #20309 wears an elegant blue gown trimmed in gold featuring a blue satin bodice with a single sheer sleeve. $75.00.

1987 Jean Barbie wears a blue denim fashion featuring a sleeveless bodice and a three-tier skirt with pink trim. A pink hairbow accents her crimped sandy blonde hair, and a blue hat completes her ensemble. $65.00.

1987 Llanera Barbie #51-0257 uses the SuperStar Barbie head mold with dark brown hair parted on her right and adorned with a white satin ribbon and violet eyes. She wears a white peasant blouse with lace trim, a pastel floral-print white tiered skirt with lace trim, and white pumps. $85.00.

1987 Amiga Barbie is identical to Llanera Barbie but she is packaged as "Barbie Tu Mejor AMIGA." $85.00.

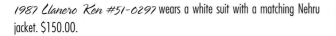

1987 Llanero Ken #51-0297 wears a white suit with a matching Nehru jacket. $150.00.

1987 *Miss Barbie* uses the SuperStar Barbie head mold with dark brown hair parted on her right and violet eyes. She wears an ivory dress featuring a lacy collar and tiered floral lace trim on the skirt, a pink satin waistband, pink pumps, and a pink "Miss Barbie" sash. $95.00.

1988 *Fun-to-Dress Barbie #51-4558* has lovely facial paint and wears a white satin hairbow and a lacy pink teddy. $28.00.

1988 *My First Ballerina Barbie* wears a pink ballet costume with tie-on skirt, armlets, hair decoration, and slippers. $45.00.

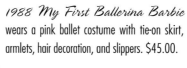

1988 *My First Ballerina Barbie* is a lovely brown-skinned doll using the SuperStar Barbie head mold with black hair. $165.00.

1988 Olimpico Ken is the only Ken doll to use the Rocker Derek head mold. He has brown skin and brown eyes. He is dressed for the 1988 Olympic games in a sweatsuit featuring white pants and a white jacket with pink sleeves, waistband, and collar or a blue sweatsuit with pale blue sleeves, waistband, and collar. Each jacket features the Olympic rings logo. Note the box photo that shows Ken doll with the SuperStar Ken head mold with pink skin. $150.00 each.

1988 Spring Time Primavera Barbie wears a romantic white ball gown with rhinestone earrings and necklace. She comes with a two-piece parasol with tulle and silver glitter. $110.00.

1989 Aniversario Barbie 1959 - 1989 is very similar to the American 1988 Happy Holidays Barbie with some differences in her dress fabric, hairstyle, and makeup, and the holly leaves and berries accents on her silver waist bow and hairbow are omitted on this Venezuelan edition. $135.00.

1989 Emerald Barbie #51-0430 wears an emerald green ball gown accented with a pink flower at the waist, a dramatic green boa, and a green "emerald" necklace and earrings. She uses the SuperStar Barbie head mold with green eyes. $100.00.

1989 Wet 'N Wild Withney #4136 wears a swimsuit featuring a lavender top with attached green bottom and a purple bracelet. She uses the Steffie head mold with brown eyes, brown skin, and black hair. Rotoplast likely misspelled Whitney when they created this unique doll. $95.00.

1990 Agua Marina Barbie #51-0452 has sandy blonde hair worn in an updo. She wears a long sleeveless white gown featuring a blue flower decoration encircled by tulle and a sky blue tulle stole. She wears a dramatic handring, earrings, and necklace featuring blue rhinestones. $150.00.

1990 Fashion Play Barbie #51-0462 has silver blonde hair and wears a red and white dress featuring a red midriff and red collar with heart designs on the white fabric. $45.00.

1990 My First Barbie #51-9942 wears a lovely blue version of the purple and white gown worn by the 1990 American My First Barbie. $35.00.

Trademarks

- Burberry®, the Equestrian Knight Device®, and the Burberry Check® are trademarks belonging to Burberry Limited.
- CHEROKEE® is a trademark owned by Cherokee Inc.
- "CK/Calvin Klein Jeans" is a logo form of the trademark owned by CKTT.
- COCA-COLA, COKE, the Dynamic Ribbon device, and the design of the contour bottle are trademarks of The Coca-Cola Company.
- Disney Characters © The Walt Disney Company.
- FASHION AVENUE is a registered trademark of Newport News, Inc., a member of the Spiegel Group.
- Ferrari product under license of Ferrari Idea S.A. All Trademark Rights Reserved. 2000 Ferrari Idea S.A.
- Oscar de la Renta is a registered trademark of Oscar de la Renta, Ltd.
- STEIFF® and the Button in Ear® are registered trademarks of Margarete Steiff GmbH.
- Wonder Woman and all related characters, names, and indicia are trademarks of DC Comics © 1999.

About the Author

Introduced to Barbie doll as a child, J. Michael Augustyniak played with his older sisters' Barbie dolls alongside traditional boys' toys such as Mego superhero dolls and the original Kenner Star Wars action figures. His most beloved childhood doll, a gift from his Grandma Clara, was the 1976 Ballerina Barbie doll, which was the first new Barbie doll Michael owned. Childhood toys are often discarded, but seldom forgotten, so Michael's love for Barbie was rekindled soon after high school graduation in 1988, when a clearance-priced Rocker Derek doll wearing a gold stage costume proved too temping to resist. At this time, Michael was working at his first job as an associate with Kohl's department store, and he marveled at how Mattel's dolls reflected current fashion trends. California Dream Ken doll's fish necktie looked similar to the novelty neckties sold at Kohl's! While briefly concentrating only on Ken dolls, the magnificence of the 1988 Happy Holidays Barbie proved irresistible, and an ensuing job at Sears prompted the collecting of Sears Exclusive Barbie dolls. Within a few years, Michael owned thousands of dolls and fashions. He has attended 13 national Barbie Collectors' Conventions since 1991.

Michael earned his bachelor's degree from Indiana University in 1992 with a double major in English and social studies, and he has continued working toward a master's degree. He put his love of writing and photography to use as a staff member of *Barbie Bazaar* magazine beginning in 1995. He also contributed to *Dolls in Print* magazine, where he collaborated on the first collectors' fashion doll photo soap opera, *Pink Intentions*, from 2000 to 2001. Michael was promoted to *Barbie Bazaar* price-guide editor in 2002 and is now considered a leading authority on Barbie doll, sharing his views on collecting with various radio shows over the years.

Michael's books include the *Barbie Doll Boom* (1996), *Thirty Years of Mattel Fashion Dolls* (1988), the best-selling *Collector's Encyclopedia of Barbie Doll Exclusives and More* (1997, 2000, 2001, 2004), *Collector's Encyclopedia of Barbie Doll Collector's Editions* (2005, 2008), and *Barbie Doll Around the World* (2007).